How to Deal with and Defeat Gang Stalkers

by

Chomi Prag

ISBN: 1500483028
ISBN-13: 978-1500483029

DEDICATION

I dedicate this book to Almighty God who has never let me down and given me strength and discernment. I also dedicate this book to my Grandpa Prag who knows what I've had to struggle with in this life, my husband, my children, my parents and sister, my Aunt Chong I and of course, my friends, Facebook supporters and Targeted Individuals all around the world.

CONTENTS

ACKNOWLEDGMENTS

I acknowledge my editor, Mr. Thomas Carney, who helped me edit my first published book, Cult of Mirrors, who helped me edit this book and witnessed the gang stalking I've suffered because since he's a targeted individual as well, Mr. Derrick Robinson founder of Freedom from Covert Harassment who is a targeted individual. Actor/ Artist Stephen Shellenberg who is a targeted individual, Ms. Kim Ange and all other targeted individuals who have reached out to offer me support. It is with your help I was able to write this book.

Friends Jennifer Vann, Matthew Plummer, Al Borg, Karen Bratonja and Steve Phillips ALL people who helped get this book out there and are strong believers in the United States Constitution. Also Matthew and Tim who greatly assisted me; these people DO work for the government. Not everyone is in on it.

CHAPTER1
THE BEGINNING

As I sit and write this book I am surrounded by a bunch of "haters" envious of whom and what I am, people who don't like what I have to say and people who don't know how to mind their own damn business. It's called "the place I live" and quite honestly it's a joke. For a long time, ever since I moved over to where I currently live and even at the last place I lived, I was a targeted individual. In this book my experiences will focus on my current living situation. I won't name names yet…in time young grasshopper...in time. I know most of the people involved and am still getting down to business. I can say the landlord (owners), neighbors next door, across the hall and downstairs as well as a so called "caretaker" have participated with the landlord to gang stalk as well as The Milwaukee School of Engineering. I've let others know who is involved in case anything happens. If you're ready to get down to business then this is the book for you!

Stay tuned for further information as to this place that you will NOT want to get involved with because they actually attempt to curtail your rights as a tenant, harass you, harass you with other tenants and the police, let strangers into your place, police without a warrant and ultimately think they as well as the other junky tenants over here are above the United States Constitution and the law. This situation is completely ridiculous and it's gone so far that my family's and my life is threatened.

These people actually went so far as to hack my computer and deleted my book from it. I was able to recover something. Therefore, the first publication and even second revisions of this book weren't good, since they weren't edited properly and were cut short because I was writing under extreme coercion, another violation of my right to Freedom of Speech under the First Amendment of the United States Constitution. Also the conditions, physical conditions, have been horrible to write under since I can't write at the place I live. My editor and I figured, if they felt THAT threatened by the book we better put something out there rather than nothing. Even this revision is written under extreme time constraints…something NO writer in the United States should have to suffer.

I was able to retrieve some parts of the book but understand these people actually took it so far as to screw up the formatting of the book as well so there are no page numbers and I can't guarantee there ever will be.

There were other formatting problems they too. They constantly track my computer use and think they know everything my editor and I know since they've been conducting illegal wiretapping, eavesdropping and hacking of my computer.

It's very normal during these kinds of circumstances to want to give up what you're doing. These gang stalkers will contact others to try to manipulate and take advantage of you during a time period where you're weak, or they think you're weak. Remember, YOU control your state of mind. People that take advantage of people during a time where others are ganging up on you are pathetic. Sure, even creditors and mortgage companies will try to do the same. Don't cave in. They're in on it too. It's normal to feel like you want to give up. Don't. It's normal when you're under extreme amounts of pressure to get upset and angry; even at your child or children and at your family; even yourself. Brush it off, take a step back and breathe. God is there to help, but you must help yourself first. Take that first step and God will be there.

Cheaters never win; it may look like they do in the beginning or to other people, even to themselves. "Don't a worry da" as my mother says. Do what you gotta do, you've got one life to live. Do it the way you want and think is best. If you need emotional support I'm here to offer that.

I invite you to like my Facebook pages to stay updated as well: https://www.facebook.com/chomipraglawoffices and https://www.facebook.com/AuthorChomiPrag .

In actuality it started a while back. Let me explain. I decided to challenge a large non-profit corporation for a young man who filed bankruptcy. I'm an attorney. I always end up helping "the little guy", I don't know why. Maybe it's because I decided to go to law school to help people. I mean, of course I have to make money too, but my intent was never to become an attorney to be rich.

I decided to help a client who hired me to handle his bankruptcy case. He was given a loan by The Milwaukee School of Engineering to go to school there. What I ended up unearthing was that this loan from the Milwaukee School of Engineering was totally and completely unnecessary in terms of this young man attending school there; meaning he already had more than enough in other student loans and paid the Milwaukee School of Engineering (MSOE) in full for his tuition and everything else before signing a loan to them. Then, to make matters worse, after signing the a loan to MSOE that paid for nothing at their school, MSOE didn't even give the kid the money from the loan back to him as a refund so he could spend it. This was basically a "phantom loan". We argued that this "student loan" was dischargeable in bankruptcy and guess what, the law supported us. I found a loophole, which is what attorneys are damn well supposed to do. My client was extremely intelligent, good looking, sharp dressed and most of all wasn't afraid of challenging authority and guess what, neither was and neither am I.

The thing with the court system and judges is that it's very political and all about who has the most money. I'm a woman, so I'm not part of the "good ol' boys" network. I don't have "political connections", I run a small law office, my family isn't college educated and I basically "come from the street". I'm not a millionaire and all I cared about with this young man was that we try to get rid of this loan because as far as we were both concerned it was fraudulent. There are two attitudes of thought about this case. One might ask, "Well, why did he sign it then?" Yes, he did sign it it's true. The other school of thought it, "Why did MSOE present him with a loan that he didn't need and which they weren't even going to give back to him?"

My client and I took the school of thought that MSOE shouldn't have presented him with a loan that didn't pay for anything at their school and which they didn't give back to him to spend. Hey, he's an 18 year old kid, inexperienced, doesn't come from an educated family and he TRUSTED The Milwaukee School of Engineering so he did whatever they said. Most people do, they don't question anything and don't question authority.

I've always been bullied, ever since I went to elementary school. I'm also a minority, since I am half Korean, half white. I have a strange name. I was mostly bullied by black boys in elementary school. So being bullied isn't something new to me. I've been used to groups of people picking on me since I was a little kid. Gang stalking is worse than bullying though because gang stalkers use illegal means to gain private information about you; eavesdrop, send people to eavesdrop, will tap and bug your land line phone, cell phone, emails, faxes and relentlessly attack you by getting people in authority positions like the police to help them. Bullying is more open, you'll know your attackers and at some point you can get away from them. Not with gang stalking. You may not be able to point your finger directly at a person or persons, it won't be straightforward and the tactics they use may or may not include social networking or the internet to bad mouth you. Gang stalking is more secretive and more advanced than bullying since electronic surveillance may also be used.

Anyways, back to the law. I can tell you one way some judges get around and skirt the substance of the law is to find ways to say you, as an attorney, didn't do this or that right.. Some judges will even cause you to lose the case or dismiss it by saying there was a procedural error or some other error or errors to toss the case right out of court. Judges are friends with other judges, so filing an appeal can be a joke too. It's just easier to say the lower judge was right, especially if they used to sit together on the same court or still do. Like a district court judge who used to sit on the lower court as a bankruptcy judge, or an appellate judge that used to sit on the same court as a trial judge. Come on, these people go golfing together, belong to the same country clubs, get coffee together, their wives are friends, etc., etc.

"Procedural error" is the simplest way for a judge to dismiss your case or to find a way to get really upset with you. Also if the judge doesn't like you and you correct the judge as to how he's WRONG they can and will sock you and or your client with hefty fines. It's the easiest way for them to side with their "friends" and protect their ego. My client and I found out, the hard way, that the United States court system isn't for people who don't have money; rather it's made for large corporations. The case became a fiasco and a big joke. But we'll save that for another day.

Even afterward, the unfairness of court commissioners and the Wisconsin Judicial Commission became all too obvious.

The Wisconsin state court system isn't any better. I've actually had a judge deny myself, my editor and the public access to crooked Milwaukee County Deputy Sheriff's personnel records, which the public is MORE than entitled to see since they pay these officer's salaries. I guess only The Milwaukee Journal Sentinel can get disciplinary/ personnel records under Wisconsin Open Records law, not the "little people". Of course, the judge claimed there was some procedural error in our request, the easiest thing for them to say in order to "toss the case" and get it out of their courtroom. (http://www.jsonline.com/news/milwaukee/supreme-court-sides-with-newspaper-in-dispute-with-milwaukee-police-department-jl5tldj-160510565.html)

You'll come to find that some judges don't want to make decisions or don't want to get in the middle if you're fighting for someone that doesn't have "political clout". Instead they'll want to force you to settle the case when that isn't what claimants should be forced to do. You do have a right to duke your case out in court if you choose; after all you do have to pay a filing fee to get a case into court at all. Some judges are afraid of big corporations and companies and they're used to dealing with prosecutors on a regular basis, since they see them sitting in their court every day. When you come in and start telling it like it is and know the law, people in the court system (judges, deputies, clerks, etc., etc.) don't "like you".

CHAPTER 2
WHEN I STARTED TO NOTICE IT

After what happened with the MSOE case I started experiencing strange things like people and the same vehicles following me around, white utility vans just showing up and parking outside where I lived or stayed, my cell phones acting funny, clicking noises around me, etc. Typical and classic signs that I was under surveillance. My husband saw it too. Now I'll admit that before the surveillance started I was hanging around with what some people may consider the "unsavory" type. But I sort of fell apart after the MSOE case because I became SO disappointed and SO disenchanted with the court system and didn't have much, if any, of a support system. It's easy to tell people what to do, but that's not real support.

Real support is going through the painful experience, at least somewhat, with the person who is suffering. I didn't have that. Everyone was busy, they had their own life, their own family, they were married...basically they weren't a victim themselves so why did they care? They really didn't. I was so naive about the court system, so the case woke me up. Lord knows court may be fair sometimes, and not other times. You may get a judge that does well for your case, you may not. It's a roll of the dice. There are other ways, besides going to court, to get that "justice". I'm not saying you can't go to court, but what I'm saying is that if you don't have money to hire an attorney, don't bother and if you don't have money to keep going with a case, like the court filing fees and to keep paying an attorney, you may be out of luck in the end. Generally speaking, judges don't like pro bono clients. You're a pain in their rear.

I worked for my MSOE client pro bono. I didn't get paid from his case. I fought a huge corporation for free because they ripped my client off and I saw that. Yes, of course I was thinking this could turn into a huge case for me too. It was an opportunity! It would have been a HUGE professional step for me, a HUGE financial opportunity and I would have created a HUGE precedence that would have helped other people. I had people around me warn me not to keep going, but I like standing up for what's right, and still do, and that was number one in my mind. It always is. I won't change that for anyone or anything so whatever, and if you're like that neither should you. I don't regret my decisions in this life, and neither should you. There is nothing to be ashamed of, no matter what. That's how people control you and that's how they can blackmail you. Forget that. The only thing you have to make right with is GOD in the end. For whatever reason you're being targeted is none of my concern, I could care less. In my opinion it is NEVER right for a group of people to get together against one person. A fair fight is one on one and, as my husband says, out in the open. But we know that gang stalkers don't do that because they are weak.

They also use underhanded tactics and illegal means to obtain information about you...to harass you. Most of all it's never one on one. Remember, that's how strong and threatening you are to them. They are so weak they can't fight you alone. You're the strong one, YOU'RE IN CONTROL.

I'm not saying ALL judges are bad people, nor am I saying ALL police are bad people, nor am I saying ALL neighbors are in on it or are bad people. Most people are weak individuals who can't stand up on their own and have to join the crowd. That's not me and never has been so I don't understand people that gang up on people. As a matter of fact if anyone ever approached me to join in and gang up on a person I would straight up say "no" and to be frank would be offended that they even approached me with it; it means you have a bad character.

But there are a lot of crooked people who have no ethics and honestly no backbone. They do what they're told. But let's be real here; there ARE crooked judges, there ARE crooked court systems, there ARE crooked cops, there ARE crappy neighbors and there ARE people who eavesdrop. Yes, eavesdrop, which is at the very least a state offense. But gang stalkers think they're above the law; in fact they will use crooked police, the landlord, other neighbors, the cable company, utility workers, and so on to try to get you into legal trouble if they can't break you in other ways like getting you to hurt YOURSELF. If you feel suicidal; STOP. My goodness, gang stalkers are downright comical. Don't be your own worst enemy. The greatest adversary against you is you and your attitudes. You're not a victim, you're in control. It may not seem like that, but you are relinquishing control when you allow them to upset you. Why bother? You DO have to develop a thick skin. See, I could care less what other people think about me. I'd be lying if I said I never cared. I mean, I used to care. But at the end of the day other people don't pay your bills and since I was slammed after the MSOE case I got tougher and guess what, people don't like that either…especially since I'm a woman. It will be your own attitude about things that controls whether you create your own prison. Really what people want is for you to kowtow to them. Get it yet? Besides, kowtowing to them means YOU are also a gang stalker and a weak, pathetic individual that they can recruit for their future projects. Are you of weak constitution? Do you have an unethical character? Are you a piece of junk?

Realize in the end it doesn't matter whether you're soft or loud, nice or mean, etc., etc. Over here it's "noise disturbances" that they falsely accuse me of. But see it doesn't matter whether I'm loud or soft, as will be discussed shortly because I'm not loud. People just listen to what I'm saying over here and they use that as "pretext" or an excuse to harass me and it led to illegal wiretapping anyways. I'm not loud; people just don't like hearing what I say, don't mind their business, are up in my stuff, are envious, or think that I should only be able to say what THEY decide I can say.

I'd better tell you something else. I'm an extremely strong believer in privacy rights and more importantly the United States Constitution including the Second Amendment, right to own and bear arms, the First Amendment, right to free speech and the Fourth Amendment right to be free from unreasonable searches and seizures (WARRANT requirement). Absolutely! In my opinion I live in the best country in the world because of these rights that I have as a United States citizen. There are people that don't like that. Believe me, there are people who will attempt to curtail your right to own a gun, your right to say what you want and your right to privacy in the place you live. My attitude is go live in China then. If you don't want to own a gun, you don't have to. But don't tell others they can't. If you don't want to say certain things because you think it's disrespectful or rude, don't. But don't tell others they can't. If you want strangers coming into your house, the police, without a warrant you go right on ahead but don't tell the rest of us that's okay.

Save your money, hopefully you have. Hopefully you've saved something for an emergency because you may well damn need it. It's not too late if you have the gumption to get up and work, even sell your plasma if you need to leave the situation, do internet work, etc. Also I hope you have at least one person that you can actually trust that is willing to help you because the advice I will eventually give you will require a strong attitude, money, good health, one good and honest, trustworthy person with an open attitude that is on your side. My advice will give you money saving tips. Understand that I am available to help you legally, in non-legal ways and also if you need emotional support, I am available to talk to. But please remember that legal services aren't cheap, they aren't cheap anywhere. I will offer you cheaper ways to deal with and defeat your perpetrators in order that you keep money in your pocket so it's not spent in a foolish way.

Remember, save for your rainy day. Don't think just about today, think about tomorrow. Also, I'm not going to deal with mind control techniques or electronic torture. I can't profess to be an expert in these areas, although I do sympathize with your situation and will try to help you in any way that I can. Also, please understand the court system may not be the best route for you, although you may think it is. I've had people contact me telling me the CIA or FBI is after them. That very well could be the case, but what makes you think these perpetrators are actually agents of the government…especially high level government like the CIA? I'm not necessarily saying they're not. But you must know something that is EXTREMELY threatening. Otherwise, let us be realistic. Your perpetrators are LYING to you. Why would you believe that they are the CIA? How do you know they are? Hopefully not just because they said so.

***__This book is designed to provide information and motivation to our readers. It is sold with the understanding that the publisher/ author/ editor is not engaged to render any type of psychological, legal, or any other kind of professional advice. The content contained is the sole expression and opinion of its author. No warranties or guarantees are expressed or implied by the content in this book. Neither the publisher/ author/ editor nor the individual publisher/ author/ editor shall be liable for any physical, psychological, emotional, financial, or commercial damages, including, but not limited to, special, incidental, consequential or other damages. Our views and rights are the same: You are responsible for your own choices, actions, and results.__ ***

However, if you are in need of legal services my office is available to be hired to represent you and/ or give you legal advice. Please visit: http://www.chomiprag.com/.

CHAPTER 3
WHAT IS GANG STALKING

Gang stalking is also commonly known as group stalking, organized stalking or mobbing and the victim of the gang stalkers is often referred to as a "targeted individual". Now let me be straight here, not everyone who claims to be a victim is. But I'm not here to judge. Some people may have mental disorders that cause them to think they are a targeted individual.

There may be evil spiritual forces at work around them as well. Nevertheless even persons that have a mental disorder who think people are after them ARE being gang stalked, by evil spirits. I'm not going to discuss how to combat those types of evil, spiritual forces in this book either. I do believe in God and I would recommend anyone to develop and maintain a relationship with God who will defend and protect you against your attackers, whether they are physical or spiritual.

I'm going to focus on human beings, perpetrators that are in physical existence. If you need spiritual guidance I am open to counseling and praying with you. I was a guest on an internet radio talk show, Talk Shoe, thanks to Mr. Derrick Robinson founder of Freedom from Covert Harassment, where a couple victims discussed bug attacks. That is horrendous and horrible but I believe that is more than gang stalking, it's spiritual stalking too, but you know your situation better than me. I think that going to church and talking to God will greatly help your situation.

Jesus Christ was gang stalked himself. I'm not telling you that you HAVE to worship God or Jesus. You can worship what you please. But I would ask that you keep an open mind about how Jesus dealt with his gang stalkers. Groups of people plotted against Him and eventually killed Him out of envy and because they didn't like hearing him tell the truth.

> **Luke 20:20-26, Revised Standard Second Version**: "20 So they watched him, and sent spies, who pretended to be sincere, that they might take hold of what he said, so as to deliver him up to the authority and jurisdiction of the governor. 21 They asked him, "Teacher, we know that you speak and teach rightly, and show no partiality, but truly teach the way of God. 22 Is it lawful for us to give tribute to Caesar, or not?" 23 But he perceived their craftiness, and said to them, 24 "Show me a coin. Whose likeness and inscription has it?" They said, "Caesar's." 25 He said to them, "Then render to Caesar the things that are Caesar's, and to God the things that are God's." 26 And they were not able in the presence of the people to catch him by what he said; but marveling at his answer they were silent."

In the end Jesus "one upped" his perpetrators and they didn't like Him because he was, by far, smarter than them. But we're not Jesus so God doesn't expect us to sacrifice our lives to gang stalkers. Gang stalkers try to one up you to gain an advantage. Jesus wasn't afraid since he wasn't doing anything wrong. If you ARE doing anything illegal I'm telling you to STOP now. It's not worth it. You have no leverage over your attackers if you are doing drugs, driving drunk, etc., etc. Also doing these things doesn't make you strong, but rather it makes you weak and you need strength during this difficult time. Those kinds of crutches don't help you in this life anyways. Stay sober, that way you can think and react quickly. You will also need to get sleep, keep up with your hygiene, clothe yourself, EAT, shower and exercise. You're going to fight your opponents; like a boxer. You have to be mentally, emotionally, physically and spiritually fit. It doesn't mean that you won't feel down sometimes because of the situation. It's not your fault people are too far up in your business. Obviously they aren't concerned with making money and taking care of their own business. These gang stalkers have nothing; they aren't successful people in life and never will be. How can they? They have nothing of value in this world because they're too damn busy watching YOU. But if you fall down, fall down by yourself and don't let others see you falling. Then get back up and FAST!

People who are successful in this life mind their business and are too busy trying to make a living and take care of themselves and their family to give a care about what so and so is doing or saying. Take it from me, I know. They're watching YOU because you are one or more of these things: God loves you, you share a special relationship with God, you're better than them, confident, popular, successful, good looking, intelligent, smart, got it together, tell it like it is, are fashionable, help others less fortunate, have an unpopular opinion, have money, know how to make money, know about money, are too smart for your own good, take care of your family, take care of yourself, know how to work hard, have a clear and excellent voice, can sing well, are musically inclined, know something you're not supposed to, seen something you're not supposed to, protect your family, protect your friends, etc., etc., etc. and in the end are ENVIOUS of you or THREATENED by you. They aren't these things and never will be. Oh well, let the talents God gave to you shine. You don't have to hold back for anyone and you're not here to make friends or kiss anyone's butt. If you've seen something or know something you're not supposed to, you may not even know it. Even if you do you won't be able to get that out of your head anyways. We'll get to methods of protection later.

Organized stalking, also called group stalking or gang stalking, is the organized targeting of an individual or couple. There are many methods used to create this targeting, but the main goal of organized stalking is to create fear in the victims. (https://www.freedomfchs.com/information/organized-stalking) Gang stalking IS stalking, by more than one person.

Stalking is defined as the "repeated harassing or threatening behavior toward another person, whether that person is a total stranger, slight acquaintance, current or former intimate partner, or anyone else." (http://criminal.findlaw.com/criminal-charges/stalking.html). Stalking is illegal.

Stalking is now on the books in every state.

Stalking laws in most states pertain to a relatively new crime involving a clear pattern of conduct in which the offender follows, harasses, or threatens another person, putting that person in fear for his or her safety. An individual may be charged with stalking regardless of any pre-existing relationship with the victim. Stalking victims can range from celebrities to former spouses who have obtained a protective order against their ex. (http://criminal.findlaw.com/criminal-charges/stalking.html)

Stalking, is a crime.

The federal government, all 50 states, the District of Columbia, and U.S. Territories have enacted criminal laws to address stalking. The legal definition for stalking varies across jurisdictions:

- State laws vary regarding the element of victim fear and emotional distress, as well as the requisite intent of the stalker.

- Some state laws specify that the victim must have been frightened by the stalking, while others require only that the stalking behavior would have caused a reasonable person to experience fear.

- States vary regarding what level of fear is required.

- Some state laws require prosecutors to establish fear of death or serious bodily harm, while others require only that prosecutors establish that the victim suffered emotional distress.

- Interstate stalking is defined by federal law 18 U.S.C. § 2261A.

(http://www.bjs.gov/index.cfm?ty=tp&tid=973)

According to the Bureau of Justice Statistics, individuals are classified as stalking victims if they experienced at least one of these behaviors on at least two separate occasions. In addition, the individuals must have feared for their safety or that of a family member as a result of the course of conduct, or have experienced additional threatening behaviors that would cause a reasonable person to feel fear.

The SVS measured stalking behaviors as:

- making unwanted phone calls
- sending unsolicited or unwanted letters or e-mails
- following or spying on the victim
- showing up at places without a legitimate reason
- waiting at places for the victim
- leaving unwanted items, presents, or flowers
- posting information or spreading rumors about the victim on the internet, in a public place, or by word of mouth.

(http://www.bjs.gov/index.cfm?ty=tp&tid=973)

Summary Findings by the Bureau of Justice Statistics report that during a 12-month period an estimated 14 in every 1,000 persons age 18 or older were victims of stalking

- About half (46%) of stalking victims experienced at least one unwanted contact per week, and 11% of victims said they had been stalked for 5 years or more.
- The risk of stalking victimization was highest for individuals who were divorced or separated—34 per 1,000 individuals.

- Women were at greater risk than men for stalking victimization; however, women and men were equally likely to experience harassment.

- Male (37%) and female (41%) stalking victimizations were equally likely to be reported to the police.

- Approximately 1 in 4 stalking victims reported some form of cyberstalking such as e-mail (83%) or instant messaging (35%).

- 46% of stalking victims felt fear of not knowing what would happen next.

- Nearly 3 in 4 stalking victims knew their offender in some capacity.

- More than half of stalking victims lost 5 or more days from work.

(http://www.bjs.gov/index.cfm?ty=tp&tid=973)

A New York attorney named Keith LaBella made a request to the Department of Justice under the Freedom of Information Act requesting the Department of Justice's results and findings of a survey they performed on Stalking by Groups or People; as contained in the Supplemental Victimization Survey (SVS) and National Crime Victimization Survey from 2006. Please see the Department of Justice's letter of response to Attorney LaBella proving he made the request, as well the results of those surveys here: (http://gangstalkingismurder.wordpress.com/foia-documents-from-dojs-office-of-justice-programs/). So when people attempt to deny that gang stalking exists, rest assured that it does.

Really, victims of any form of stalking are suffering from harassment. Of course, there are many different levels of harassment. To harass is defined as 1. to disturb persistently;

torment, as with troubles or cares; bother continually; pester; persecute. 2. to trouble by repeated attacks, incursions, etc., as in war or hostilities; harry; raid. (http://dictionary.reference.com/browse/harass).

The more your stalkers see you as a threat the higher the level of harassment you will suffer. Whistleblowers will face gang stalking frequently because of the knowledge they possess about illegal activities in an organization which they reveal to the public. Basically, they're a threat.

A whistleblower is "anyone who has, and reports, insider knowledge of illegal activities occurring in an organization. Whistleblowers can be employees, suppliers, contractors, clients or any individual who somehow becomes aware of illegal activities taking place in a business either through witnessing the behavior or being told about it. Whistleblowers are protected from retaliation under various programs created by the Occupational Safety and Health Administration (OSHA) and the Securities and Exchange Commission(SEC)." (http://www.investopedia.com/terms/w/whistleblower.asp).

Whistleblowers are well known, and are often given protection by the government, whereas victims of gang stalking may not be taken seriously or have a higher threshold to meet by the government in order to receive any sort of protection whatsoever. If you mention "whistleblower" people will know what you're talking about. Mention "gang stalking" and you'll run across blank looks on people's faces. Remember, in the end you protect yourself, and you have a right to protect yourself and your family. Waiting on any form of "government" is a waste of time. You have to fight back and show that you're unafraid. You don't necessarily have to be confrontational, but maybe that's your style. Either way I'm going to show you different ways to combat your attackers.

You might wonder, are you being stalked? Am I being harassed? Is there a difference between the two?

> Harassment is repeated unwanted contact, so STALKING IS HARASSMENT, but that doesn't mean harassment is "stalking". Someone can harass you by being annoying/ pestering, mean, obnoxious or by just being an outright "jerk", but if the harassment doesn't make you "afraid", then it is not considered "stalking".

However, harassment can quickly turn to stalking when the actions become extreme.

(http://poshbytori.hubpages.com/hub/Am-I-Being-Stalked-Signs-of-Stalking-Harassment)

Some ways to tell you're being stalked:

- The sense you are being watched and followed everywhere you go and even where you live

- People around you pay attention and listen to everything you do and say

- You have a sense that there is NO PRIVACY in anything you do, whatsoever

- You notice consistently rude behavior from people you don't know or others for no apparent reason and staring directed in your vicinity, at you, at your property or where you live/ stay

- You hear excerpts from conversations you had in the privacy of your home coming from people around you

- You feel that those around you have access to your communications

- **Financial toll.** A stalking victim may need to take time from work to change a phone number, move, replace damaged property, obtain a restraining order or testify in court. Of the 79% of stalking victims who were employed during the 12 months preceding the SVC interview, 1 in 8 lost time from work. 130,000 victims reported that they had been fired from or had been asked to leave their jobs because of stalking.

  (https://www.privacyrights.org/are-you-being-stalked)

- Relationships and friendships become distant or strained for no apparent reason

- You experience problems on the job where groups of people are plotting to have you terminated (workplace mobbing)

- Business deals consistently fall through for no apparent reason

- You experience vandalism on a regular basis

- You notice that your things are not in the same place you left them when you left home or some small items may be missing

- Frequent car repairs

- Staged car accidents

- Street theater skits where they play out some sort of scenario that feels threatening to you in some manner

- Frequent appliance or electronic malfunctions

- People call the police on you and try to get you into trouble

- People spread bad, nasty and untrue rumors about you.

https://www.privacyrights.org/are-you-being-stalked)

Various forms of harassment:

Electronic

Electronic harassment is the alleged use of electromagnetic equipment to harass a victim. Psychologists have identified evidence of auditory hallucinations, delusional disorders or other mental illnesses which can result from electronic harassment.

Landlord

Landlord harassment is the willing creation, by a landlord or his agents, of conditions that are uncomfortable for one or more tenants in order to induce willing abandonment of a rental contract. Such a strategy is often sought because it avoids costly legal expenses and potential problems with eviction. This kind of activity is common in regions where rent control laws exist, but which do not allow the direct extension of rent-controlled prices from one tenancy to the subsequent tenancy, thus allowing landlords to set higher prices. Landlord harassment carries specific legal penalties in some jurisdictions, but enforcement can be very difficult or even impossible in many circumstances. However, when a crime is committed in the process and motives similar to those described above are subsequently proven in court, then those motives may be considered an aggravating factor in many jurisdictions, thus subjecting the offender(s) to a stiffer sentence.

Mobile

Mobile harassment refers to the sending any type of text message, test, photo message, text message, sext, photo message, video message, or voicemail from a from mobile phone that causes the receiver to feel harassed, threatened, tormented, humiliated, embarrassed or otherwise victimized. It is a form of cyber bullying.

Online

Whereas content may be offensive in a non-specific way, harassment directs obscenities and derogatory comments at specific individuals focusing for example on gender, race, religion, nationality, sexual orientation. This often occurs in chat rooms, through newsgroups, and by sending hate e-mail to interested parties (see cyber bullying, cyber stalking, hate crime, online predator and stalking). Any comment that may be found derogatory or offensive is considered harassment.

Police

Unfair treatment conducted by law officials, including but not limited to excessive force, profiling, threats, coercion, and racial, ethnic, religious, gender/sexual, age, or other forms of discrimination.

Power

Power harassment is harassment or unwelcome attention of a political nature, often occurring in the environment of a workplace including hospitals, schools and universities. It includes a range of behavior from mild irritation and annoyances to serious abuses which can even involve forced activity beyond the boundaries of the job description. Power harassment is considered a form of illegal discrimination and is a form of political and psychological abuse and bullying.

Psychological

This is humiliating, intimidating or abusive behavior which is often difficult to detect leaving no evidence other than victim reports or complaints. This characteristically lowers a person's self-esteem or causes them torment. This can take the form of verbal comments, engineered episodes of intimidation, aggressive actions or repeated gestures. Falling into this category is workplace harassment by individuals or groups mobbing.

Community-based Harassment — stalking by a group against an individual using repeated distractions that the individual is sensitized to. Media reports of large numbers of coordinated group stalking individuals, individuals stalking victims, including a press interview given by an active duty police lieutenant, having described this community-based harassment as gang stalking.

Racial

The targeting of an individual because of their race or ethnicity. The harassment may include words, deeds, and actions that are specifically designed to make the target feel degraded due to their race or ethnicity.

Religious

Verbal, psychological or physical harassment is used against targets because they choose to practice a specific religion. Religious harassment can also include forced and involuntary conversions.

Sexual

Harassment that can happen anywhere but is most common in the workplace, and schools. It involves unwanted and unwelcome words, deeds, actions, gestures, symbols, or behaviors of a sexual nature that make the target feel uncomfortable. Gender and sexual orientation harassment fall into this family, involving children [in sexual antics], calling someone "gay" or "homo" [can be] a common insult falling into this category. The main focus of groups working against sexual harassment is protection for women, but protection for men [has come] to light in recent years.

Workplace

Workplace harassment is:

- the offensive, belittling or threatening behavior directed at an individual worker or a group of workers

- odious dealing through pitiless, malevolent, hurtful or embarrassing attempts to undermine an individual worker or groups of workers.

Recently, matters of workplace harassment have gained

interest among practitioners and researchers as it is becoming one of the most sensitive areas of effective workplace management. In Asian countries, it attracted lots of attention from researchers and governments since the 1980s, because a significant source of work stress is associated with aggressive behaviors at [the] workplace. Third world countries are far behind oriental countries in that there are limited efforts to investigate the questions on workplace harassment. It is almost unseen and the executive leaders (managers) are almost reluctant or unconscious about it in the third world countries. Under occupational health and safety laws around the world, workplace harassment and workplace bullying are identified as being core psychosocial hazards.

(http://en.wikipedia.org/wiki/Harassment)

Various methods used in organized stalking:

- **Brighting**: having people turn on their headlights everywhere you go, especially parking lots and side roads. [Also, **flashing red laser type dots** into or around the area where you're at.]

- **Harassment**: Neighbors making lots of extra noise seemingly on-purpose. Leaving notes on your door. Calling the police on you for false complaints.

- **Following**: Vehicles or pedestrians following on the road, sidewalks, and in stores -- following can be in front as well.

- **Yard**: People running into the yard to create noise or leave strange items.

- **Noise**: Car horns, fireworks, gunshots, door slamming, electrical yard power tools like lawn mowers, ringing your doorbell, standing outside your place of residence making noise.

- **Mobbing**: Having people or cars surround you

instantaneously.

- **Airplanes**: flying over the place you stay at apparent timed intervals.

  (https://www.freedomfchs.com/information/organized-stalking)

- Illegal wiretapping, eavesdropping and "bugging" around you, the place you live in or places around the place you live or work.

- Illegally trying to evict you.

- Attempts to evict you.

- Attempts to "cheat" you out of money.

- **Gaslighting** or **gas-lighting:** (1) a form of mental abuse in which false information is presented with the intent of making victims doubt their own memory, perception, and sanity. Instances may range simply from the denial by an abuser that previous abusive incidents ever occurred, up to the staging of bizarre events by the abuser with the intention of disorienting the victim. (http://en.wikipedia.org/wiki/Gaslighting)

- **Same Time Entry/Exit**
  When entering or leaving your home, is one of your neighbors there waiting and then entering or leaving his home at the same time. Ex. Pulling into your driveway, then a neighbor already sitting in his car starts pulling out of his driveway.
  (http://www.urbandictionary.com/define.php?term=gang%20stalking%20methods&defid=1637242)

- **Public rudeness / Anchoring**
  Do you get rude stares, bumps or unexpected actions or

> talk from people you do not know or strange chat from strangers on the internet like they know you? In Gang Stalking, Anchoring is used to make the target have fear with things happening in daily life that others consider to be normal. That can be done with frequent demonstrations. The key is the frequency just like other Gang Stalking methods. For example, people show you a pen everywhere you go, and their attitude is rude or crazy against you. You don't know them. You just wonder what's going on. Imagine that happens everyday, for a week, for a month, for a year. That makes you have fear with a pen. In this case, a pen is ANCHORED with your state of fear. It can be anything. A cell phone, notebook computer, a medical mask, clothes of the same color, anything. (http://www.urbandictionary.com/define.php?term=gang%20stalking%20methods&defid=1637242)

There are different levels of gang stalking as well; from the not so severe to the downright dangerous. **In reality the downright dangerous can include attempts to get you into legal trouble, attempts to kidnap you and attempts to kill you and/ or your family.** I've had contact with one specific gang stalked victim "Mike" who informed me his dog "Silver" was poisoned by his attackers, his so called "neighbors". Your attackers may try to hurt, kidnap or even KILL your children. They want to hurt you and/ or the people or things you love and care about and they may and WILL use any means necessary to do so. There are detrimental effects that victims of stalking and harassment suffer.

The goal of perpetrators of this GANG STALKING is to:

- Cause a target to lose their mind

- Cause a target to be mentally committed

- Cause a target to go to jail or prison

- Cause a target to commit suicide

- Cause the financial downfall of a target

- Cause a target to be depressed
- Cause a target to lose their reputation
- Cause a target to lose family and friends
- Cause a target's relationship to fall apart; cause the breakup of relationships as well as marriage
- DO ANYTHING that causes detriment to the target and/ or the target's family and/ or the things or people the target loves or cares about
- Kidnap you and/ or your family
- Kill you and/ or your family.

Effects of Harassment

There are physical, emotional, mental and behavioral symptoms you, as a victim, will suffer from being harassed.

Physical
Headaches
Frequent infections
Taut muscles and Muscular twitches
Fatigue
Skin irritations
Breathlessness

Emotional
Loss of confidence
More fussy
Irritability
Depression
Apathy
Alienation
Apprehension
Anxiety

Mental
Worrying
Muddled thinking
Impaired judgment
Nightmares
Indecision
Negativity

Behavioral
Accident prone
Loss of appetite
Loss of sex drive
Drinking more
Drug use
Insomnia
Restlessness
Smoking more
(http://www.targeted-individuals.com/#/symptoms-of-harassment/4568080185)

Effects of Stalking

Some people won't reach out to obtain help from being stalked for one or more of the following reasons:

- Not understanding what is happening to them is stalking and/or illegal
- Trying to pretend that it isn't happening
- Believing they should be able to deal with the situation, thinking the stalker will see reason, or not wanting to get the stalker into trouble
- Fear that others will think they are over-reacting or they will be blamed for somehow having encouraged the stalker in the first place.
- Fears about how the stalker will respond either to them or those that they love or care for
- Direct threats from the stalker
- Feeling isolated in their plight, believing there's nothing

that can be done to help them, or not knowing who or where to go to for help
- Previous requests for help being ignored
- Fear of losing their job or the situation becoming worse when the stalking originates in the workplace
- Financial limitations in regard to seeking legal advice or taking time off to seek help
- Limited options in respect to changing their situation e.g. relocation to safer housing
- Language barriers. (https://www.stalkingriskprofile.com/victim-support/impact-of-stalking-on-victims)
- Not knowing what to do
- Think they should get along with the stalkers; or KOWTOW (http://dictionary.reference.com/browse/kowtow)

I didn't even know what "gang stalking" was the first time was around. All I knew was that a caravan of people were "out to get me". Look, if you're as sensitive as I am it won't take much to realize that something very weird is going on around you, that people are out to get you and that electronic harassment is being used against you. Even if you're not a sensitive person eventually you'll become aware of the gang stalkers tactics and activity. After seeing these strange things occurring, like your phone having problems, people following you, your computer being hacked, people making noise where you live, etc, etc. you'll finally be convinced that you are being gang stalked. After realizing to myself that it WAS happening to me the first time I started poking around on the internet, I can't remember what exactly I searched, but I found the term "gang stalking". You don't have to have solid proof to know within yourself that it's happening to you. YOU KNOW THE BEST. Also, it's not your JOB to have to convince people of anything. If you know then that's what matters. God knows anyways.

Being stalked by one person is scary enough, but when you have more than one person stalking you...an actual GROUP of people how the hell are you supposed to feel? How about threatened? Is that how you feel?

Mental

- Denial, confusion, self-doubt, questioning if what is happening is unreasonable, wondering if they are over-reacting
- Frustration
- Guilt, embarrassment, self-blame
- Apprehension, fear, terror of being alone or that they, others or pets will be harmed.
- Feeling isolated and helpless to stop the harassment
- Depression (all symptoms related to depression)
- Anxiety, panic attacks, agoraphobia (frightened to leave the house, never feeling safe)
- Difficulty concentrating, attending and remembering things
- Inability to sleep – nightmares, ruminating
- Irritability, anger, homicidal thoughts
- Emotional numbing
- Symptoms of Post-traumatic Stress disorder e.g. hyper vigilance (always on the lookout), flashbacks of frightening incidents, easily startled
- Insecurity and inability to trust others, problems with intimacy
- Personality changes due to becoming more suspicious, introverted or aggressive

- Self-medication alcohol/ drugs or using prescribed medications

- Suicidal thoughts [and ideation] and/or suicide attempts.

Physical

- Fatigue from difficulty sleeping, being constantly on guard, symptoms of depression

- Effects of chronic stress including headaches, hypertension

- Gastrointestinal problems

- Fluctuations in weight due to not eating or comfort eating

- Development or exacerbation of pre-existing conditions e.g. asthma, gastric ulcers and psoriasis.

- Dizziness

- Shortness of breath

- Impact on health of increased use of alcohol, cigarettes or drugs

- Sexual dysfunction

- Physical injury due to not concentrating or being under the influence of substances

- Heart palpitations and sweating.

Effects on social life, work and school

- Insecurity and inability to trust others impacting on current and future relationships and friendships

- Problems with physical and emotional intimacy
- Avoidance of usual activities e.g., going to the gym, going out
- Isolation through trying to protect others, feeling misunderstood or psychological symptoms
- Others withdrawing from the victim because they don't believe the victim, they are unable to cope with the victim's mental state or as a direct consequence of third-party victimization
- Victim moving to a new area, changing their phone number, name or even their appearance
- Deteriorating school/work performance
- Increased sick leave
- Leaving job or being sacked [fired]
- Changing career
- Dropping out of school – poorer education and career opportunities.

Effects on finances

- Loss of wages due to sick leave, leaving job or changing career
- Costs incurred through legal fees
- Expense of increasing home and personal security
- Cost involved in repairing property damage

- Seeking psychological counseling and medical treatment
- Cost involved in breaking leases on rented properties
- Expense of relocation.

(https://www.stalkingriskprofile.com/victim-support/impact-of-stalking-on-victims)

CHAPTER 4
MY EXPERIENCES THE SECOND TIME AROUND

The sign at the hospital I went to have my ultrasound the other day read "The expert at anything was once a beginner". I'm pregnant with my second child and due any day now. These losers actually pick on a pregnant woman with a small child. President Rutherford B. Hayes came up with that quote, "The expert at anything was once a beginner." My editor said he was called "President RutherFRAUD Hayes". HA! I try to keep a sense of humor about things, and so should you. I know it can be easier said than done. It's hard to laugh when you're surrounded by "haters" and people constantly spying on you or if you feel your life or the lives of people you love or care about are in danger. But I would try to encourage you to take a step back and laugh about something. Laughter is excellent medicine for anyone. Let me tell you about my experiences this second time around, it may make you laugh. Hope it does!

I notice that no matter where I go people pay attention to me anyways. It's funny, when I want attention I don't get it but when I don't want it it's all over the place and all over me.

But gang stalking is different than just attention, it's very negative attention centered and focused on one person or a couple. It's very hard to live past this kind of extremely negative attention. But you have to. You really have to not care about what other people think or say about you. You can't please everyone and why would you want to anyways? It's called YOUR LIFE. Even if you've made mistakes so what. EVERYONE HAS and no one is perfect. Maybe people are picking on you because you committed an illegal act that they think deserves gang stalking. I remember the first time around asking the "unsavory type" guy I was seeing whether anyone deserved that kind of treatment from people… "gang stalking". He answered with "pedophiles". I told him that no one deserves to be gang stalked for any reason. Let the courts decide the ACCUSED pedophile's fate. Another thing I've learned is that the court isn't always right either. There are innocent people sitting in jail or prison, wrongfully convicted. My editor and I have been wrongfully accused of things in the court system we weren't guilty of as well. I've been accused of things I'm not guilty of in the court system too. It's very easy to have people say you're guilty and with the bang of a gavel you've lost your life.

Police, firefighters, utility workers, neighbors, landlords, bosses, co-workers, so called "friends" and even sometimes so called "family" can participate in gang stalking against you, along with many others. If you have never seen the movie *The Lottery* I would strongly recommend you watch it here:
(http://www.youtube.com/watch?v=pIm93Xuij7k) [part 1]
(http://www.youtube.com/watch?v=PMhV3fwx5Sg) [part 2].

Does that look familiar to you? Are you living through it? The problem is that people that participate in gang stalking are weak minded people that don't know how to stand up for what's right and not join the crowd. They're just happy it's not happening to them. The majority isn't always right.

There's an experiment that was performed by Mr. Stanley Milgram, a psychologist. It was a study based on obedience to authority and how most people will simply "do as they're told".
(http://www.youtube.com/watch?v=fCVlI-_4GZQ)

> The experiments began in July 1961, a year after the trial of Adolf Eichmann in Jerusalem. Milgram devised the experiment to answer the question 'Could it be that Eichmann and his million accomplices in the Holocaust were just following orders? Could we call them all accomplices?' (Milgram, 1974). In Milgram's experiment 'The learner (a confederate called Mr. Wallace) was taken into a room and had electrodes attached to his arms, and the teacher and researcher went into a room next door that contained an electric shock generator and a row of switches marked from 15 volts (Slight Shock) to 375 volts (Danger: Severe Shock) to 450 volts (XXX).' (http://www.simplypsychology.org/milgram.html)

Milgram was testing his subjects on the subject of obedience and whether they would just follow blind orders.

> Participants were 40 males, aged between 20 and 50, whose jobs ranged from unskilled to professional, from the New Haven area.

At the beginning of the experiment they were introduced to another participant, who was actually a confederate of the experimenter (Milgram). They drew straws to determine their roles – leaner or teacher – although this was fixed and the confederate always ended to the learner. There was also an "experimenter" dressed in a grey lab coat, played by an actor (not Milgram).

Two rooms in the Yale Interaction Laboratory were used - one for the learner (with an electric chair) and another for the teacher and experimenter with an electric shock generator.

The 'learner' (Mr. Wallace) was strapped to a chair with electrodes. After he has learned a list of word pairs given him to learn, the 'teacher' tests him by naming a word and asking the learner to recall its partner/pair from a list of four possible choices

The teacher is told to administer an electric shock every time the learner makes a mistake, increasing the level of shock each time. There were 30 switches on the shock generator marked from 15 volts (slight shock) to 450 (danger – severe shock).

The learner gave mainly wrong answers (on purpose) and for each of these the teacher gave him an electric shock. When the teacher refused to administer a shock and turned to the experimenter for guidance, he was given the standard instruction /order (consisting of 4 prods):

Prod 1: please continue.

Prod 2: the experiment requires you to continue.

Prod 3: It is absolutely essential that you continue.

Prod 4: you have no other choice but to continue.

(http://www.simplypsychology.org/milgram.html)

Sixty five percent of participants continued to the highest level of 450 volts and ALL the participants continued to 300 volts.

(http://www.simplypsychology.org/milgram.html)

There are criticisms of Milgram's Experiment. The first criticism is that there were over seven hundred participants in the study and that the sixty five percent of participants who gave an electric shock to the learner were actually a smaller sample than the full seven hundred people who participated in the experiment.

> Over 700 people took part in the experiments. When the news of the experiment was first reported, and the shocking statistic that 65 percent of people went to maximum voltage on the shock machine was reported, very few people, I think, realized then and even realize today that that statistic applied to 26 of 40 people. Of those other 700-odd people, obedience rates varied enormously. In fact, there were variations of the experiment where no one obeyed.

(http://www.npr.org/2013/08/28/209559002/taking-a-closer-look-at-milgrams-shocking-obedience-study)

The next criticism of Milgram's Experiment is that it was "unethical" meaning that the participants weren't told the truth about the experiment. "Certainly for people in academia and scholars the ethical issues involved in Milgram's experiment have always been a hot issue. They were from the very beginning. And Milgram's experiment really ignited a debate particularly in social sciences about what was acceptable to put human subjects through." (http://www.npr.org/2013/08/28/209559002/taking-a-closer-look-at-milgrams-shocking-obedience-study)

The final summing up of the criticisms and critiques of Milgram's Experiment are succinctly put in an answer posed on Wiki Answers.

> Milgram's experiment was unethical for a number of reasons. Firstly, it used deception, with the participants not being aware of the true nature of the study. Secondly, it didn't give a clear right to withdraw: if

> participants were hesitant, they were verbally prodded into continuing. Finally, there was some harm to the participants. All of them experienced stress and one even suffered convulsions. There have also been questions over the value of the study. Mandel has claimed that it lessens the evil of something like the holocaust, by appearing to take responsibility away from the NAZIs. (http://wiki.answers.com/Q/Why_was_milgram%27s_experiment_unethical)

Nevertheless, I believe the Milgram Experiment shows the kind of society we live in. People just do what they're told and that's why it's so easy for these gang stalkers to form a screwed up community where they actually think it's okay to form a group to harass a single person or couple. Nevertheless, who cares why people do these kinds of things. We're here to make sure you can survive your situation because it doesn't have to be like this for you. You have to fight back to combat this sort of unfairness. So before I show you how to deal and combat it I'll tell you about what I myself have experienced where I currently live. Where I live people have the impression that they can do unto others what you should not do unto them, as if they're above reproach. The very people trying to get you into trouble are the people who surround you. Of course you're going to feel threatened and constantly vigilant.

Here's a laundry list of things I have suffered from at the hands of my attackers: severe harassment by the "neighbors", "owners/ landlord", "caretaker", mail theft and attitude by the US Postman about it, illegal wiretapping and eavesdropping and illegal and unlawful entry by the police into my place of abode without a warrant because the "caretaker" gave them keys, amongst other things. I'll describe more about this shortly. The people next door like to chat it up with their gang stalking "buddies" across the hall, the people directly downstairs like to hang around their porch to harass our comings and goings and listen to everything we do, they all talk it up amongst themselves and help each other out in the unit. Of course, they're ALL gang stalkers, they're all friends!

You can generally tell when people don't know how to mind their business. That's how it started over here. I could tell people were always paying attention to what I was doing and saying, etc. Since they don't respect the law, they obviously can't be trusted therefore it's very dangerous over here. There's a "building caretaker" who has the keys to every single person's place and unit and he lets the police in without a warrant even after the owners were warned through me that the "cops don't get in without a warrant" MONTHS ago. The owners don't even disclose this "caretaker's" last name and for all we know his first name isn't even accurately given by the landlord. The "caretaker's" phone number is traced to the landlord and his real name is being hidden and undisclosed, even though he lives on the premises. This guy has the keys to your life, yet every other tenant who lives here has their last names blasted all over the boards in the front of their unit, which they never even asked tenants' permission to disclose. But somehow the "caretaker" is above it all. His last name is more important than everyone else's since it isn't disclosed anywhere, not the board in front of the unit he lives in and not on any paperwork from the landlord whatsoever.

But eventually things escalated to a point where enough was enough, which is why I decided to write this book. I knew people were paying attention to what was going on, but it went further than that. The first "real" incident of there being a problem was when I suffered mail theft. I put a couple packages in the wall mount flip top mailbox that's downstairs in the common hallway that looks kind of like this

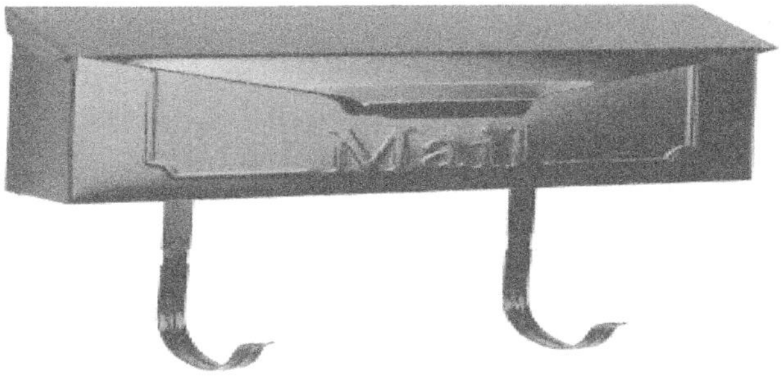

That mailbox is the mailbox for the unit and yes, it is a United States Postal Service mailbox. There is a little sign on the box that says "outgoing mail" and the mailman picks the mail up from there regularly; it's part of his route.

Therefore, according to 18 U.S. Code § 1705 - Destruction of letter boxes or mail...

> Whoever willfully or maliciously injures, tears down or destroys any letter box or other receptacle intended or used for the receipt or delivery of mail on any mail route, or breaks open the same or willfully or maliciously injures, defaces or destroys any mail

> deposited therein, shall be fined under this title or imprisoned not more than three years, or both.
> (http://www.law.cornell.edu/uscode/text/18/1705)

I contacted the local post office and even left a note downstairs asking the mailman, in a polite manner, as to where the packages went since they were down there and I saw them before he picked up the mail and they were gone after he came to pick up the mail. This US Postal Mail Carrier actually left a note back to me in the individual mailbox that he had no idea where the packages went but said I was supposed to be using the address of the unit as the return address rather than an office or mailing address.

To which I filed a mail theft report because he's obviously a bozo, who walks around wearing a miner's hat, to deliver mail and likely threw my mail away or stole it…or a neighbor did. Take your pick. You can use ANY return address and place that piece of mail in ANY United States Postal Service (USPS) mailbox in the country, you don't have to put your mail ONLY in a USPS Mailbox that is within the zip code or vicinity of your return address. See the purpose of a return address. (http://pe.usps.com/businessmail101/addressing/returnAddress.htm)

Fine, alright so I lose money from that. But now I don't trust the mail service so I have to go mail things physically somewhere else and I surely don't get mail delivered here. That also costs more money for me. I know I can't trust leaving any mail in the building at all.

Next there is a sign that says there are security cameras in the basement. I had been wondering where these were so I asked the "caretaker" who answered "there aren't any". Before asking the "caretaker" this question we asked the landlord where the security cameras were, they said "they're inoperable". Which one is it? Let's make up our mind.

I've dealt with constant noise disturbances : heard people argue in here, sure have, pound up and down the stairs, hang around by my door, yell and holler, lots of door slamming, CONSTANT DOOR SLAMMING, talking outside where I live, ringing my doorbell, etc., etc. But since I'm of the attitude that I should mind my business, I do. I'm too busy with my own problems to care about anyone else's. Fireworks, kids yelling outside, kids jumping up and down on their pogo stick right by the window and etc, etc. The whole nine yards! These are CONSTANT noises by other people and of course they can do things we're not supposed to. It's really about unfairness and being treated unequally.

I can't help if people listen to what the hell goes on in MY ABODE and don't like it. They aren't supposed to be listening anyways; you'll see the eavesdropping laws soon enough. So they "don't like me". Whatever. It's not their place to judge because they should be minding their own business. It's not because anyone's loud, it's just because they're listening to things that are supposed to be private. It's ridiculous.

The tenants refuse to empty the lint trap from the dryer which poses a fire hazard. I finally got sick of cleaning up after these people and complained to the landlord. After all there is a sign that says you're supposed to empty the lint every time you use it. Obviously people can't read or think other people should clean up their messes. Based on this occurring over and over again I complained and yet still kept cleaning their messes, a filthy, dirty lint trap. I became concerned because of my being pregnant and my small child so I called the fire inspector because I am positive that there are years of accumulated crap in that dryer and why should we burn up over here because of that or them? The fire inspector said they would come out nonetheless, but I could tell they were friends with the landlord too. A couple days later someone was out there banging around in the dryer because they had to clean it. This is when trouble started.

Also I don't call in repairs often; there are many different safety hazards here. I'm not trying to be a nag. But when a repair is needed we get attitude from the landlord or repair person who make the excuse that we broke it or we're loud, etc, etc. so just forget repairs, also threatened with eviction.

Some "neighbors" left a note on the door, and so has the landlord, complaining about noise and THREATENING that they would call the police and threatening about domestic violence. Remember, we're in our abode. Also, they'll claim I have a loud voice and, etc., etc. That's just a lie because it doesn't matter whether I'm soft or loud as you'll see since even whispering, talking normally and discussing things has led to illegal wiretapping and methods of eavesdropping. You'll soon see that this is just pretext as an attempt to evict and gouge money. These people just think they should be able to tell me what to say and what to think. This is a total infringement on my first amendment right to freedom of speech and they have actually enlisted the help of people I have been paying for services or about to do business with. Needless to say I will not be recommending these people or businesses to anyone. After all I actually had dealings with them and they're unethical to say the least.

After getting the nasty harassing letter from the "neighbors" we left a note that we apologized, even though we didn't feel we had to. Didn't matter because I could tell certain people here were very envious anyways. In turn we called the landlord informing that the "police do not get into our place without a warrant" and the landlord was also asked how they knew if drawers were being slammed in here or if we were "noisy". They replied with a "we send the 'caretaker' to your apartment to find out." You actually send the caretaker to eavesdrop? How do you know what's going on in here, what's being banged, whether it's your property being banged or mine? It's more than eavesdropping; they're all in on it over here. Yup, that's right!

I knew these people were listening to E V E R Y T H I N G up here. It didn't matter, it was ridiculous. I mean normal conversations to anything and EVERYTHING at all. When I had visitors over they were all watching, listening to what they said over here, watching out their peepholes, listening at their walls and doors even when I spoke on the telephone. Watching me from their decks, even looking at my place all the time, from inside, from outside. I had a friend come over and talk about personal legal and family matters and they were listening to everything she said. I didn't want anyone over after that.

After rent is paid there is usually some sort of threatening letter left by the landlord on the door, under the door, in the door; all the time.

Of course there are nasty stares, etc. incidents in the basement, etc. I could care less since these kinds of things don't bother me it just lets me know they're in on it too and it's not just people in the unit but others in the whole building complex as well as people nearby.

It got to a point where I called 911 and hung up. The cops came anyways and knocked on the door and don't ask me who let them into the unit because it wasn't me. My child was in the living room and I was talking with my spouse in the bathroom. Before you know it there are flashlights around in my abode flashing around the hallway and lo and behold the cops are in my abode WITHOUT A WARRANT. Needless to say they eventually left and nothing happened. But I know they were on my computer too, which I told them to stay off of. I had my husband call the landlord just to see about the eviction process since the cops were here and the landlord didn't know I called 911. There were no exigent circumstances and no emergency that would carve an exception to the warrant required by police to enter the place where you live, your abode. Didn't even hear a "knock and announce" by the police.

Needless to say my son goes EVERYWHERE with me in here now. I'm so sorry to my son that I left him out in the living room while talking to my husband in the bathroom and strangers entered the place where I live. I am so sorry to my son. I'll never let that happen ever again in my life. Things have really changed around here. Windows are kept locked and shut. I take my child everywhere with me all the time.

Of course some other kind of nasty letter was left by the landlord about curing the noise within 5 days, because they didn't know I called 911. Remember, I hung up and didn't speak to anyone at 911. I knew the landlord would be chomping at the bit to try to evict us but just kept the fact that I called 911 and hung up before talking to anyone at 911 to myself. Wanted to see where this went.

Under federal and Wisconsin law you don't have to open the door for the police; UNLESS they have a warrant. [Make sure to check your state laws]. In fact you shouldn't. But when the police were here that's all they kept preaching was that we should have. So even the police have the attitude that you must let them into where you live if you call 911 but hang up and speak to no one at 911. But that's just not the law. Also the police seem to think if they come and knock on your door you have to let them in, which is also not the law. Understand, even without a warrant if you stand there with an open door and say the cops can't come in without a warrant they'll do it anyways. Then you can fight about it later in court and hopefully you or someone else didn't get arrested and hopefully you or someone else didn't have anything ILLEGAL and hopefully you or someone else aren't sitting in jail or prison because the "fruit of the poisonous tree" doctrine won't be used until after you've been sitting in jail and blah, blah, blah. You should check out these websites because the advice is priceless in regards to the warrant required by police to enter where you live. This is reflected in the Fourth Amendment to the United States Constitution. Unless the police can prove there was an emergency they can't enter where you live without a warrant unless YOU let them in. (http://www.flexyourrights.org/faqs/police-at-my-door-what-should-i-do/) Another good place to visit is: (https://www.aclu.org/drug-law-reform-immigrants-rights-racial-justice/know-your-rights-what-do-if-you)

Nevertheless mind you, if the police want to they'll get the keys from the "caretaker" over here and come on in, WITHOUT A WARRANT anyways. Obviously it isn't safe here. If the "caretaker" will do that to us what makes you think he won't do that to you, or worse? It would be very easy for someone to come in here and plant something illegal and then call the cops on us. What about that? These tenants that participate with the landlord actually gang stalk us and WE'RE supposed to feel safe? Well, we don't. Obviously strangers are let into our apartment without our permission so I'm sure that they've come in here when we haven't been here too and since the neighbors are in on it we'll just be "outta luck". If these other tenants were smart they would take a step back and think to themselves that could be them, and even worse that they know nothing about a "caretaker" that has access to their life…their children's lives. But instead they've all ganged up on us over here.

A couple days later the blinds fell in a room, the windows were open and I called out for my husband's help. Of course SOMEONE called the cops and they were back over here. This time I just let them in, didn't know what the hell was going on and just wanted to tell them whatever and get them out. They weren't rude or anything and not all the police were rude the first time either. They said the place has thin walls and they said they would report their coming up to the abode to the landlord. I'm standing there thinking "what the hell for?" I just wanted them in and out and I already knew they would come in just by getting the keys so I didn't feel like I had a choice. Something you should never do. So I'm expected to curb my constitutional rights over here which can't keep going on. Of course, the landlord and tenants here got cop friends too. I knew they were looking for an excuse to evict and they found it.; a second time the police were over.

Another letter was left by the landlord, mind you I'm 7 or 8 months pregnant at this point, chomping at the bit to give another reason to evict. Remember, I never said that I was the one that called 911 the first time and hung up.

I had enough so a letter had to go out on my letterhead because it was obvious that the police were being used as pretext to make my family and myself homeless and to try to evict us. I had enough and said what needed to be said in regards to legal rights we have.

Next my computer began acting up; Malwarebytes stopped working completely and things started appearing on my computer that I didn't put there and things disappearing on my computer. Needless to say I had to hire a computer expert to get down to business with my computer. See how these things cost me money, cost me time, etc., etc. They try to make you destitute. This is classic gang stalking 101.

Since then and even before then I've said things, even whispered, in the abode that HAVE OBVIOUSLY BEEN MISCONSTRUED. No one is yelling, no one is talking loud, nothing just having normal conversation, praying to God, etc., etc. and still they'll say I have a loud or am shouting, etc. anyways. That's not it, these people think they should pick and choose what you can and can't say. You can laugh loud, but not talk loud. You can joke loud, but not argue. You can argue, but only the way they think you should and what they think you should. You can talk, but only what they decide is okay. My right to Freedom of Speech under the First Amendment to the US Constitution is walked all over there.

I can also tell that my Second Amendment right to keep and bear arms is also threatened because I guess people think because they are anti gun you have to be too. I DON'T THINK SO. The Second Amendment to the United States Constitution gives every citizen this right, the right to keep and bear arms. As if I'm here to prove something to them. I'm not here to win a popularity contest. The rent is paid and we mind our own so leave us alone. It's not our fault you eavesdrop, which is illegal.

Now the illegal wiretapping starts. There are at least 2 witnesses to this that have been on the landline phone with me that have experienced the amateurish b.s. tapping of the phone line. First it started with television/ cable interference. One particular channel, channel 108 Sprout. It's all I really watch over here. Because these tenants are so far up my business they even know what we watch on TV over here so they began interference with the cable. First we noticed that channel 108 wasn't working. All other channels seemed to be working but channel 108.

I called Time Warner who tried rebooting the box. Rebooting wasn't working like it normally should. The television was taking too long and doing nothing. Finally we got the channel back. The funny stuff moved to the land line phone, which is also connected to the cable. Squealing, amplified sound, echoes on the phone, static, scratching, popping, humming and even more so while hanging the phone up on the hook. We noticed it but let it go a few days. I've been on the phone discussing personal financial matters with a financial advisor, talking to my parents, talking to a friend, etc., etc. Everything normal people do. Now all these people know all my business.

Fine, now I've had it because it's gone on for a couple days now so upon hanging the phone on the hook I announce: "Illegal wiretapping is a federal offense and so is eavesdropping…also a state offense". WHOOPS! I know everyone, including definitely the tenants next door (that we heard become disgruntled by my loud comment) heard me, along with the tenants downstairs and the ones across the hall. I picked up the phone and it was clear as a whistle. They all had their "pow wow" earlier in the day. I called Time Warner Cable to have someone come out, but of course when they came all was fine and I had to remind the service person that "I sure hope Time Warner Cable isn't illegally wiretapping our phone without a warrant". Ever since then the atmosphere has changed. But I don't feel safe here AT ALL. It just went from one for of illegal wiretapping and eavesdropping to another.

Of course these people are a joke. I'm at this place by myself most the time, almost all the time with my son and I'm set to give birth shortly. I know that while the phone was being illegally tapped I called my doctor's office and sent an important fax all which have been intercepted as well. It isn't hard to intercept a fax. "Fax machines have proliferated to almost every business and many homes. This method of communications is one of the most easily and successfully targeted. The means for intercepting fax signals are the same as for telephones..."
(http://www.wright.edu/rsp/Security/V2comint/Fax.htm)

Then they moved to my cell phone. It kept turning off constantly so that got sent back to the cell phone carrier since it's obvious that the cell phone has been tapped as well. I mean, constantly the cell phone was turning off even after I turned it back on this after they stopped on the landline.

Move forward to a few days later, now one specific car follows us from the grocery store where a worker there talks about calling the police while shopping in the store. That's called "anchoring", as discussed earlier.

The computer had to go back to be repaired AGAIN another bill. They know our financial situation. They hacked into my computer again. I had seen it going on for a while but didn't have the time to deal with it. But it had become too much and I had to find the money to take the computer to an expert once again to have it cleaned and yes, it had been hacked.

We are forced to live out of a car and spend barely any time there now because it is that unsafe, this is called homelessness even though the rent has been paid. No computer use shall be conducted there again either. But even so, they're still tracking my computer activity and attempted to stop the publication of this book by actually deleting it from my computer. They were saving it to an "application link" internet file. So they had access to much more than just that on my computer. I was able to recover some of the book, but it hasn't been written or edited the way it should have been and that's because even while I was in the computer store they sent their private investigator in to snoop around and try to check what I was doing in there, tried looking at my computer and then gave some phony bologna story about looking for surveillance equipment. Give me a break folks.

CHAPTER 5
SIGNS YOU'RE UNDER SURVEILLANCE

Because I already have experience with being a targeted individual who has been under surveillance before the things that have gone on where I currently live make me laugh. Don't get me wrong, it's not fun to go through these things in life and I'm not trying to say your situation is funny or trying to make light of it. I just think it's funny that people think they can one up you by using illegal, underhanded tactics and by ganging up on you. It's not a joke over here where I live and I am very concerned for my family's and my safety; very much so.

For starters I'm an attorney. I speak to clients, potential clients, email them, do research for clients, etc., etc. So wherever I go there's my office and wherever I am, as long as it isn't in public, there's my office. I take privacy matters VERY seriously. My client's privacy is of utmost concern to me and being able to speak in privacy about my own personal matters is as well. I have lost money and financial opportunities because of the loss of privacy I have suffered here. My health and my family's health have suffered. Obviously, because I have to fight these gang stalkers I lose time to make money and end up spending money to combat these fools. It's a necessary evil. Living out of a car is homelessness. They know these are the extreme situations they have put us through, yet still my editor and I decided to publish our unfinished and unedited drafts since it's better than nothing to help people. Every day we try to update the book because our goal is to help people and we've gone to great lengths to get the book published, including people following us around, being homeless and getting ready to welcome a new baby. Our goal is to help people.

There is absolutely no privacy there whatsoever and it's been like that for some time now. I can't even go to the bathroom in privacy. Absolutely nothing I do over there is private and it's been like that for a long time. I've suffered alone and by myself for quite some time as well. Illegal wiretapping isn't all that's involved. Most importantly where I live there has been a constant attempt to curtail and erode my US Constitutional Rights including coercion and deletion of the book itself. Writing this book has been incredibly difficult, if not next to impossible and they know that. They know the handicaps I am working with; yet still I will carry my son and heavy bags up stairs to get my work so I can get this information out to you.

I can't talk to friends, talk on the phone, go to the bathroom, take a shower, invite friends over, talk to clients or potential clients without someone listening over here. Basically I can't do a darn thing without people paying attention to what I'm doing.

There are different methods employed by gang stalkers to harass you. These include wiretapping, eavesdropping, bugging, foot and vehicle surveillance (being followed), and hacking of the computer.

Eavesdropping

What is eavesdropping? "To listen secretly to a private conversation." (http://dictionary.reference.com/browse/eavesdropping)

"Eavesdropping is secretly listening to the private conversation of others without their consent, as defined by Black's Law Dictionary." (http://en.wikipedia.org/wiki/Eavesdropping). Eavesdropping can also be done over telephone lines (wiretapping), email, instant messaging, and other methods of communication considered private. (If a message is publicly broadcast, witnessing it is not considered eavesdropping.) VoIP communications software is also vulnerable to electronic eavesdropping via infections such as Trojans.

What the people over here will try to claim is that they can hear everything anyways because they can hear me out their window, etc. It's not "thin walls" either. No siree; these neighbors actually go out of their way to hear what's going on over here. They actively do it. Thin walls, hearing someone out their window, etc. doesn't matter.

The crime of eavesdropping means to overhear, record, amplify or transmit any part of the private communication of others without the consent of at least one of the persons engaged in the communication, except as otherwise provided by law [,p]rivate communications that take

place where one may reasonably expect to be safe from casual or hostile intrusion or surveillance[. B]ut such term does not include a place to which the public or a substantial group of the public has access. A person commits the crime of criminal eavesdropping if he intentionally uses any device to eavesdrop, whether or not he is present at the time.
(http://definitions.uslegal.com/e/eavesdropping/)

If you are out in public, and that isn't where you live inside your abode, and you announce or say something don't expect to be able to use "eavesdropping" as a way to say someone was in your business, basically.

A person can violate eavesdropping statutes by doing the following:

1. Unlawfully intercept or procure another to unlawfully intercept a wire, oral or electronic communication;

2. Unlawfully disclose the contents of an electronic, oral or wire communication;

3. Unlawfully use the contents of an electronic, oral or wire communication; and

4. Unlawfully advertise, sell or possess an "electronic, mechanical or other device(s)" which, by its design renders it primarily useful for the surreptitious interception of electronic, oral or wire communications. Evidence of communications obtained in violation of these statutes may be suppressed at proceedings and persons illegally obtaining them are subject to lawsuit and/or removal from their position.

(http://definitions.uslegal.com/e/eavesdropping/)

So whatever excuse people try to use, the things you discuss in the privacy of where you live or where privacy can be expected, which is basically anywhere but out in the open, are private no matter whether someone hears them or not. It's illegal for ANYONE to try to use what they overheard by eavesdropping against you.

Wiretapping

"Wiretapping" technically refers to a process where one party secretly listens to the conversation of another party over a telephone line, fax machine, computer or other communication device. Before the 1960s, police were not required to obtain a warrant before eavesdropping on a conversation. However, the Supreme Court determined that individuals have a reasonable expectation of privacy in their phone conversations and that police must obtain a search warrant before wiretapping. (http://www.legalmatch.com/law-library/article/wiretapping-laws.html)

Unlawful eavesdropping and wiretapping

It is illegal to eavesdrop and wiretap without a warrant. Are we clear on that? The Fourth Amendment to the United States Constitution protects you from unreasonable searches and seizures, without a warrant. Generally speaking unless one person that participated in the protected communication CONSENTS to the eavesdropping and/ or wiretapping or there is a WARRANT issued by a court of law allowing the eavesdropping and/ or wiretapping it is ILLEGAL.

Federal law; 18 USC § 2518 (8)(d) provides the procedure for interception of wire, oral, or electronic communications. (http://www.law.cornell.edu/uscode/text/18/2518). Federal law; 18 USC § 2511 titled Interception and disclosure of wire, oral, or electronic communications prohibited provides penalties for illegal and unlawful eavesdropping and wiretapping. (http://www.law.cornell.edu/uscode/text/18/2511)

State laws also protect a person from illegal and unlawful eavesdropping and wiretapping. Here I will just discuss the State of Wisconsin's laws, but your state has something similar as well. Wisconsin Statute 968.30 provides the procedure for interception of wire, electronic or oral communications. (https://docs.legis.wisconsin.gov/statutes/statutes/968/30?view=section)

Wisconsin statute 968.31 titled Interception and disclosure of wire, electronic or oral communications prohibited provides penalties for illegal and unlawful eavesdropping and wiretapping. (https://docs.legis.wisconsin.gov/statutes/statutes/968/31?view=section)

Warrant rules are the same under Federal law as Wisconsin law for wiretapping and eavesdropping. Legal wiretapping/ eavesdropping can

only be performed for 30 days. The 30 days starts from the time law enforcement begins the legal wiretapping/ eavesdropping or at the most 10 days from the time the warrant was ordered. Legal wiretapping/ eavesdropping occur ONCE the order granting the warrant is entered. Law enforcement can get an extension for another 30 days upon expiration of the warrant, every 30 days, by going before the court and reapplying for the warrant.
(http://www.law.cornell.edu/uscode/text/18/2518)
(https://docs.legis.wisconsin.gov/statutes/statutes/968/30)

If an application is made to the court to obtain a warrant to wiretap/ eavesdrop and it's denied the court has to inform you of such within 90 days of the application. But if the court granted the warrant the court has to inform you of the existence of the warrant within 90 days after the legal wiretapping/ eavesdropping has ended.
(http://www.law.cornell.edu/uscode/text/18/2518)
(https://docs.legis.wisconsin.gov/statutes/statutes/968/30)

CLUES YOU'RE UNDER SURVEILLANCE

PLAY GAMES

One VERY common thing you can do to find out if people are listening or watching you when they claim they're not, or claim there aren't any cameras or listening devices or pretending there aren't any is to do or say something and see what happens, see if it comes out into the open. Watch for people's reaction. For instance, say you're going to do something and see how people around you react. Do something and see if someone reveals that which you've done. Say something and see how people react. See if you get those nasty stares! You can have some fun with surveillance if you don't take it too seriously. I've been doing this over here for a while and I had no idea my words were as important or taken as seriously as the words of the Lord in the Bible. See if your secrets come out into the open, whether people disclose things that you thought were private. Like I said, try to keep a sense of humor about you. What do you have to lose?

IRREGULARITIES WITH ELECTRONIC EQUIPMENT

Radios with sudden unexplained interference, at home or in your car, is a common sign that surveillance devices are operating on frequencies close to radio bands. Interference with your television as well; one channel or multiple channels not working. Static on the television is also another tell tale sign that there's some type of covert surveillance being performed on you and in your vicinity.

> Your television has suddenly developed strange interference. Television broadcast frequencies are often used to cloak an eavesdropping signal, but such devices also tends to interfere with television reception (usually a UHF channel). Televisions also 'suck in' a lot of RF energy and because of this are very sensitive to any nearby transmitters (this is technically called Bandwidth, and TV signals use a lot of it). A small hand held television with a collapsible antenna may be used to sweep a room. Carefully watch for interference around channel numbers 2, 7, 13, 14, 50-60, and 66-68 as these frequencies are very popular with eavesdroppers. This was true when signals were analog, and even [truer] today with terrestrial broadcast TV using digital signals.
> (http://www.tscm.com/warningsigns.html)

LANDLINE PHONE

Common clues that will reassure you that you are in fact the target of surveillance will include and start with irregularities in a landline phone or other electronics' performance. Strange noises on your landline phone can be a sign of a wiretap or bug. What kind of strange noises you ask? Let's put it this way, if your phone is acting "different" from the way you're used to hearing it, chances are someone or some people are listening to your conversations on that phone and around that area, in fact even when you hang the phone up, depending on the bug or tap, its range is LIMITLESS. As my editor reminded me, there are even satellites in space that can track you and your every move. (http://www.globalresearch.ca/big-brother-spying-on-americans-the-threat-of-satellite-surveillance/21433)

That means whoever is listening can hear every single thing going on in the next room, in all the rooms! Popping, clicking, humming, static, beeping, squealing, screeching and scratching are typical observations. Strange sounds coming from your phone and volume changes can also alert you to covert eavesdropping methods being used against you. Sometimes, your phone will make sounds seemingly on its own when it's on the hook. These can be signs of an eavesdropping device that allows another person to listen to conversations in the room even when the phone is not being used and has been placed back on the hook.

> You have noticed strange sounds or volume changes on your phone lines. This is commonly caused by an amateur

eavesdropper when they attach a wiretap, or activate a similar listening device. Surveillance devices often cause slight anomalies on the telephone line such a volume shift or drop-out. Professional eavesdroppers and their equipment usually do not make such noises; so if this is going on it could indicate that an amateur eavesdropper is listening in. On the other hand you could simply be experiencing a flaw in the line, but you should check it out.

You have noticed static, popping, or scratching on your phone lines. This is caused by the capacitive discharge, which occurs when two conductors are connected together (such as a bug or wiretap on a phone line). This is also a sign that an amateur eavesdropper or poorly trained spy is playing with your phone lines.

Sounds are coming from your phone's handset when it's hung up. This is often caused by a hook switch bypass, which turns the telephone receiver into an eavesdropping microphone (and also a speaker). There is probably somebody listening to everything you say or do within twenty feet of the telephone (if this is happening).

Your phone often rings and nobody is there, or a very faint tone, or high pitched squeal or beep is heard for a fraction of a second. This is an indicator of a slave device, or line extender being used on your phone line. This is also a key indicator of a harmonica bug, or infinity transmitter being used. Of course it may also be nothing more than a fax machine or modem calling the wrong number.

You can hear a tone on your line when your phone is on the hook (by using an external amplifier). To check for something like this you would have to obtain a "recorder starter" interface (with a VOX option), or some kind of a high gain audio amplifier such as a uAmp or Kaiser 1059. Then with the phone hung-up listen to your telephone wiring. If you hear a faint solid dual tone it is a dead giveaway of someone using a "slave" eavesdropping device on your (or one of your neighbors) telephone lines. Such devices create a "command tone" when the subject hangs up the phone (so you must ensure that all of your phones are hung-up). On an added note: the most common command tones for illicit eavesdropping devices are 2100 Hz and DTMF-C, but any tone combination may be used.

(http://www.tscm.com/warningsigns.html)

CELL PHONE

In this day and age a lot of people only have a cell phone, those are subject to covert surveillance as well. If you have a hard time turning your cell phone off by pressing the "off button"; meaning the cell refuses to shut down when you turn it off, chances are it's bugged. The only TRUE way to turn your cell off is to remove the battery. If your cell lights up when it's not in use watch it, that's also a telltale sign that it's bugged.

Other signs include:

- Phone shutting down by itself
- Hot battery
- Decrease in battery life
- Background noise while on the cell
- Strange texts
- Increased data usage
- Connections to the internet when you aren't on an internet plan
- Beeping noises.

In the end you'll know. If your cell is acting or behaving differently than previously chances are it's bugged.

You should password protect your cell phone and always turn it off when not in use. When you turn it back on you have to enter a password to use the phone. This way other people can't add an application onto your phone that allows them to spy on you when you're not around it.

If your cell phone is bugged, going to your cell phone carrier may not help. I know US Cellular was in on the bugging of my cell phone in the past and they had me doing the "run around" because I was going back to their store for new phones which I was entitled to under my contract. Instead they refused to give me another new phone because; well they were in on it too. If you suspect your cell phone is bugged you can go to your carrier and request a new phone or ask they reset the default or factory settings.

Personally, as a targeted individual myself, I recommend pay per minute phones anyways. If your phone starts acting weird throw it away and get a new one. You can transfer minutes to the new pay per minute cell phone and don't use the cell phone for much of anything except for what you don't care becomes public and for emergencies. Your location can be found when you have a cell phone, period.

If you're big into technology understand that GPS systems, smart phones and all that fancy technology makes it easy to track you. Go buy a map and use that, put some phone books in your car and use a cell phone that has NO internet capabilities on it, if you must.

AT YOUR RESIDENCE OR PLACE OF WORK

How can you tell if your residence or office has been bugged? By staying aware of your environment. Oddities, like a break in without items being stolen. Just look around you. Do things "feel" strange? If things have been moved from its original position and you didn't move them, or someone you know didn't move them, then how did it wind up somewhere new? It didn't walk over there by itself. It's because someone's been in your place. The gang stalkers need to hide the bug somewhere.

Electrical wall plates are "hot spots" for covert surveillance. Small dime sized, quarter inch round, discolorations in the wall or on the ceiling can alert you to a covert surveillance device like a pinhole microphone or hidden video camera. Bumps or discolorations in the baseboard of the floor should put you on notice that your place is bugged. If smoke detectors, signs (like "exit" signs, "no smoking" signs, "restroom" signs, "elevators" signs), sprinkler heads, clocks, lamps or things with a somewhat shiny surface, have been moved or have been installed out of the blue be on the watch; these likely have bugs in them.

Drywall dust, dust or debris on the floor next to the wall is another giveaway that you're the subject of covert surveillance. Cracked, chipped, damaged ceiling tiles that weren't cracked or chipped before should also put you on red alert that there's a bug that's been installed.

New items showing up at your place or gifts given to you such as: stuffed animals, mirrors, lamps, small TVs, boom boxes, CD players, desk radios, alarm clocks, pens, markers, briefcases, calculators, "post-it" dispensers, power adapters, pagers, cell phones, cordless phones, clocks, radios, lamps, Lava Lamps, flowers and plants given in pots or baskets, picture frames, birdhouses, boxes of tissue, gym bags, purses, electrical outlets, Phillips head screws, buttons, eyeglasses, all can easily contain a covert surveillance device including a hidden video camera.

Door locks being stuck or jammed can also alert you that the lock has been picked or wielded in some manner. "Try to always use biaxial locks with sidebars (such as ASSA or Medeco). Also, only use double sided deadbolts in all doors, and good quality window bars on all windows, and a good quality door bar on all doors not used as a primary entry doors. Also, always have a quality alarm installed that contains vibration sensors on the door as well as door-open switches. (http://www.tscm.com/warningsigns.html)

SERVICE PEOPLE, TRUCKS, UTILITY WORKERS, MAINTENANCE WORKERS, SERVICE AND DELIVERY TRUCKS, MARKED AND UNMARKED TRUCKS AND VANS

When service people, including cable, utility and maintenance workers show up when you didn't call them, perk up. When service and delivery trucks, marked and unmarked trucks and vans appear and also stick around, parked nearby with seemingly no one inside this should also alert you that you are being monitored. Those ladders on top of their trucks or vans are being used to disguise surveillance equipment. Be aware that your phone company, cable company, etc. could be in on it too. Let me tell you, if you didn't call in for service don't let the service person or repair person in, including the cable company, telephone company, etc.. Also if the service or repair person doesn't have the standard uniform on bearing the symbol of the company you called in for service or the vehicle they're driving doesn't, don't let them in either.

They'll even go so far as to fake a power outage, utility outage, phone outage, etc., etc. Hey! If you don't see other "neighbors" around you affected by a power outage and there's been no big storm that caused a power outage and these "service" people show up, whether identified or not, don't let them in. They're there to install bugs or do something worse. I'd rather live without power than something even worse.

Time Warner Cable hires independent contractors that they keep NO RECORD of. That's right! Time Warner Cable hires independent contractors that will come over to do “repairs” and if you call later to ask who was over they'll tell you they don't know and have no record of the visit. Basically, if you didn't call in the repair don't let them in. If they have no identification proving they work for the company they claim and they don't have on the standard uniform for the company and/ or aren't driving a marked company vehicle don't let them in.

You wouldn't let a complete stranger into your house would you? Why do you trust them? You shouldn't. BETTER SAFE THAN SORRY. How do you know this person isn't there to hurt you? How about kill you or your family? Take care of yourself, cops aren't going to save you and neither are your “neighbors”. **They're all in on it.**

USE AN AM/ FM RADIO AS A METHOD OF DETECTION FOR LISTENING DEVICES

One excellent tool to check and verify that covert surveillance is being used is with the use of an AM/ FM radio. First of all it's legal; second of all it's cheap! Part of the problem with hiring a “surveillance expert” or private investigator to perform a sweep is that there are hand held bugging devices and other bugging devices that can be turned on and off. See the picture for an example. It is much easier these days for people to use these kinds of devices rather than risk breaking and entering into your abode to plant a bug, although this does occur. If your neighbors are in on it then your landlord or their maintenance worker coming into your place to plant a bug isn’t and won't be a problem. But still, it's much more work to plant a bug and risk criminal charges rather than to just use a hand held bugging device.

A person can point these listening devices where they want to hear what they want, when they want. It can be turned on and off at their will. It isn't always on and most of these kinds of devices are what's used today. So hiring an expert to do a sweep could be a useless waste of money where they find nothing since the gang stalkers bugging you will probably turn it off when your “expert” arrives anyways, right?

Even your car radio can be bugged. When your car radio starts behaving in a manner differently from what you're used to and things are getting “weird” you know you're bugged. Your car radio's antenna may be, and often is, exploited by an eavesdropper. When that happens, the eavesdropping may interfere with radio reception. Be on the outlook if your vehicle's radio suddenly starts getting weird. Clicks inside your car aren’t good either.

HOW TO USE YOUR AM/ FM RADIO AS A BUG DETECTING DEVICE.

Many amateur and spy shop eavesdropping devices use frequencies within or just outside the FM radio band, these signals tend to drift and will "quiet" an FM radio in the vicinity of the bug. Look for the transmissions at far ends of the FM radio band, and at any quiet area within the FM band. If the radio begins to squeal then slowly move it around the room until the sound becomes very high pitched. This is referred to as feedback detection or loop detection and will often locate the bug. The "stereo" function should be turned off so the radio is operating in "mono" as this will provide a serious increase in sensitivity. If you find a "squealer" chances are you are being spied on and at that point you can decide whether to hire a professional or not.

HOW TO USE A FLASHLIGHT TO FIND A HIDDEN VIDEO CAMERA

A video camera and its lens can be hidden but the lens can't be covered, or it won't work. The lens could be the size of a pinhole to a small nail or screw head to the size of an "o". Sometimes these spy cameras click or make noise when you walk by. Physical inspection is best to find a hidden camera. Hidden video cameras can be turned off at will too so why bother hiring an expert if you can do it yourself and save some money by using non-high tech devices?

Turn the lights off in the room you'll be inspecting. Walk around the room and see if you can see any small red or green lights or any sort of glare from an LED light or display. Now take your flashlight and shine it around and across the room and surfaces of the room. The lens of the camera will reflect the flashlight's light back at you. You can do a more advanced flashlight technique to detect hidden video cameras with a flashlight, clear red plastic, tape and toilet paper roll. (http://www.youtube.com/watch?v=vtLguXvhyzU)

Here you can see what it will look like if you find a hidden video camera using the reflection from your flashlight. The flashlight's reflection will bounce back to you from the lens of the hidden camera. (http://www.youtube.com/watch?v=fuZIC9R82-M)

COUNTER SURVEILLANCE EQUIPMENT

If you can afford it counter surveillance equipment will save you the hassle of having to make your own equipment and you can take it on your travels. (http://www.gangstalkingvictims.com/gang-stalking-victim-help)

FOOT AND VEHICLE SURVEILLANCE

You should always vary your routine, period. You shouldn't ever take the same way home, the same way there, the same way, the same time, the same this, the same that. Vary your routine and start now. That which is more convenient for you makes it easier to target and follow you. Use different bus stations, grocery stores, laundromats, etc. and at different times and days.

When you see the same vehicles or people around you and everywhere you go, or practically everywhere you go know you're being watched. Many times foot and vehicle surveillance is performed on you at the same time in conjunction with one another. When you park your car and get out of your car the vehicle surveillance will stop and that's when the foot surveillance takes over. Gang stalkers are some pitiful people. In my experience there won't necessarily be two people in their vehicle following you, although if the government is watching you this is HIGHLY likely.

If vehicle surveillance is being used the vehicle won't stand out in the crowd. By checking your rear view and side mirrors see if the same car or cars follow your driving pattern. When you get the suspicion someone is following you make sudden turns (4 right turns in a row) to confirm your suspicions. Make u-turns, try to time your driving so you make it through a yellow light as it's turning red and see if they follow you through a red light. Watch to see if they make sudden lane changes to keep up with you. If someone is following you in a car they'll break the law to keep up with you...unless other gang stalking "friends" are also tailing you. So do the same thing with the second car too when you lose the first one. This is a method of intimidation and harassment they use against you, of course. Motorcycles can also be used to follow you.

If you can't get rid of them turn into a BUSY gas station or public area. Go somewhere BUSY and PUBLIC and I don't necessarily mean Wal Mart's parking lot either or a shopping mall. Don't go to a big parking lot. You need some place with witnesses; don't trap yourself into a dead end or no through street or even an alley. Gang stalkers don't want to get caught.

If you're on the freeway and notice only one vehicle is following you get off and back on the freeway. See if the vehicle following you does the same. If a "team" of stalkers is following you on the highway then STAY ON THE HIGHWAY, do not get off. If there are a lot of other cars driving on the highway pull over to the side of the highway in the emergency lane and make a cell phone call. Your gang stalkers will drive by because it's too obvious to stop behind or around you, but they could be waiting at the next exit…so don't get off.

ALSO, DO NOT GET OUT OF YOUR CAR PERIOD. You are weaker on foot than in your car. You also have the option to SLOW DOWN and see if your followers do the same.

I don't trust the police; they could very well be in on it too. But if the situation becomes life threatening I have to tell you to call 911 so there's a record and police are sent to help you. What if you're being tailed by law enforcement themselves? Not ALL law enforcement will know whether you're under police surveillance so calling 911 will lead to the cops backing off the chase. If it's federal or state undercover police following you the local police that will be sent to respond to your 911 call won't likely know so this can cause the chase to stop and at the very least if it's your gang stalkers or a private investigator they may get into serious trouble.

If you're on foot you're in a weaker position and this is the truth. You should try to completely eliminate being alone ever. Always be in a public area around other people. I understand it's impossible to be around other people all the time, but you should try to eliminate being alone. So here are some tips in case you're caught alone on foot.

GET TO A PUBLIC AREA IMMEDIATELY. You need to know if you're in fact being followed. On the way to the public area you're thinking of, cross the street and pick up the pace. See if your perpetrator does the same. Don't blatantly turn around, even though you are tempted to do so. I've made that mistake myself. It makes it too obvious that you suspect someone is following you. If you ARE in a public area and feel safe enough drop something behind you and turn around to pick it up and look to see who's behind you; make a SERIOUS mental note of the people or person behind you, pick up your item and keep moving along.

No matter whether it's day or night don't trap yourself into a dead end or no through street or even an alley. Go towards a PUBLIC place, a busy street, coffee shop, restaurant, etc., etc. Don't run up the stairs, unless it's your only option since you're trapping yourself.

If this person or people still follow you across the street and also pick up the pace or even if you suspect someone is following you go ahead and RUN to a public area, or towards other people for heaven's sake and SCREAM FIRE. Who cares how you look. You could always call the police for help, but they may try to say you're nuts and institutionalize you as well. The legal standard, at least in Wisconsin, to institutionalize you is "whether you're a harm to yourself or the public". That doesn't mean the cops can't accuse you of being a harm to yourself or the public based on ANYTHING AT ALL and YES, you'll wind up in the mental institution. But after you're there you have to go to the court and it will have to be proven you are in fact a harm to yourself or the public. If the foot chase puts you in danger call 911. I don't trust the police because they can be in on it too and they may be TRYING to make you look nuts. Run towards a public area first and get amongst witnesses. If you know for sure someone or some people are following you run towards and into a public area and scream. Who cares what people think or what you look like. Save your own life because no cop is going to do that for you anyways. Better to be in a mental institution than dead.

You need to gain physical space between you and your gang stalker(s). If you see they have a gun run in crooked lines, not a straight line. Gain distance between you and your gang stalkers. You don't want to be in a position where you are trapped and a weapon can be used against you or a weapon is used to order you into a vehicle. UNDERSTAND THIS, if you get into the vehicle you're DEAD. That's the way you should look at it. Better fight for your life with your two feet on the ground; don't get in that car they're ordering you into. Forget that. Always lock your car doors, always lock where you live; doors, windows, basement windows and if you have a cellar door make it very secure. If you're driving and someone punches through your car window to get in and jumps in your car are you ready to floor it? You're DEAD anyways if you obey their orders.

You may not want to hear these things, but these are the kinds of situations you may find yourself in. Do you want to be killed or are you ready to take control of your OWN life? This is the situation some gang stalked victims are in. PROTECT YOURSELF, no one is coming to save you. NO ONE is going to risk their life for you. Also, are you going to KOWTOW to your attackers and perpetrators? If so then this book isn't the right "how to" for you.

For some people this is the stuff movies are made of. Yeah, it's fun to sit there with a box of popcorn and soda and watch your favorite movie stars playing out some fake rolls on the movie screen. But their life isn't really in danger. The movies are fake. Your life isn't. Only YOU know your situation better than anyone else.

COMPUTER SURVEILLANCE

Try not to download "free" programs on the internet. I'm not saying all of them are bad, but most of them contain viruses, TROJANS, that are used to monitor your computer activity.

Two good and free computer software programs I would recommend you download and use would be Microsoft Security Essentials (http://microsoft-security-essentials.todownload.com/?lp=adwords&kw=Microsoft%20security%20essentials&mt=e&ad=36775328358&pl=&ds=s&gclid=CIqu0pu4y78CFehcMgodpxMACg), and Malwarebytes (https://www.malwarebytes.org/), which you also will have to manually update. Understand that no computer anti virus or malware program is 100% accurate or going to catch everything, or protect your computer from being hacked and then hijacked and spied on.

When you download ANY programs choose the "custom" rather than "automatic" or "recommended" option to install. Pay close attention to what you're installing. Don't install additional toolbars or antivirus programs. Just install that which you requested to be installed and that's it. You have to watch this because if you don't uncheck these other boxes for stuff you don't want installed on your computer you could be opening yourself up to serious computer problems as well as hacking and hijacking.

If you've allowed remote assistance or remote access to your computer you MUST change those settings immediately. I'm not professing to be a computer expert, but let me tell you how to do that in Windows 7. First find out which version of Windows you have.

In the Start menu, right-click on "Computer." Then Click "Properties" to open the System Properties window. If it's Windows 7 proceed below.

In this same "System Properties" window follow these instructions to disallow remote access. On the left hand side click "Remote Settings". Under the "Remote" tab uncheck "Allow Remote Assistance connections to this computer", then go the box below titled "Remote Desktop" and click the option "Don't allow connections to this computer". Click the "apply" button, then click the "OK" button.

If you have a different operating system please Google how to disable or disallow remote access on your computer and follow the instructions provided.

You may wish to also disable your IP webcam which can be used to spy on you, or any webcam at all. You can always put a piece of masking tape on top of your IP webcam, which is the webcam that came on your computer.

You should also password protect your computer so that a password is required to start the computer. Shut down the computer after use or lock it when you aren't around and then require a password to be used to start up, unlock or turn the computer on. Please Google how to do this as many of you probably have different operating systems.

Now back to the signs your computer has been hacked and hijaked; meaning someone is spying on you through your computer.

SIGNS OF A HACKED/ HIJACKED COMPUTER

- Browser settings changed without your permission. Like your homepage has changed and or default search engines have changed when YOU didn't change them

- New programs or files on the computer you didn't install

- Passwords changed on the computer

- Email contacts get emails from your email account, which haven't been sent by you; change your password for that email account immediately

- Slower internet connection than usual

- Computer is generally slower than normal

- Your computer prompts access to programs you don't even know

- If you're using a modem the computer is dialing to the internet on its own

- You are unable to control the cursor on your computer screen, unable to control the mouse and the cursor moves on its own.

If these things are happening with your computer STOP using your computer and shut it down. I would highly recommend you get out your local Yellow Pages and find a computer expert in the area to help you immediately, IN PERSON. I DO NOT RECOMMEND using a computer services provider that can help you over the phone/ internet using remote access because you don’t know if you can trust them or not so let’s stay away from remote access of your computer period. Call Mr. John Roman of The Computer Market because I used him and trust him. Please contact him for computer help. 2267 S. 108th St., West Allis, WI 53227; telephone number 414-328-9000 and at email TheComputerMarket@ATT.net.

CHAPTER 6
HOW TO DEAL WITH GANG STALKERS

First off, you have to have thick skin. Second, stay healthy in your mind, body and soul. Be pissed for a little but then let it GO. Let the negativity go back to the fools that are gang stalking you.

Lookie here, these people have been listening to EVERYTHING and I mean everything from private conversations, SEX, potty time, my being sick during pregnancy, throwing up, how often I'm urinating, what I say to my child, how often I'm going poop, how many poops, anything that's been said (most of which hasn't even been true), passing gas, etc. I've even heard them make comments about the things that have been said in MY residence, as if they're participating in OUR personal stuff. They give their opinions about us. SHALL I GO ON? I guess they can't afford a television. Then they don't like our private stuff so they gang up on us because they think they're the judge and jury. Believe me, no one would want to live here and a person can only take so much of this gang stalking. So we understand what you're going through. They've been on my computer too, it's ridiculous. I even do marketing for others on the computer, keep expenses on the computer, etc., etc., etc.! Lots and lots of business matters. Needless to say the computer stays away from there period.

They always try to find an excuse to point their finger at you; this gang. So no matter what, don't blame yourself. Ask for God's help and shield yourself with positivity. Watch a funny movie, the more positive you are the better you'll be. YOU MUST PUSH THE NEGATIVITY AWAY! Even I have to work on that over here because all these gang stalkers are negative. There's more negativity than positivity geared towards my family and myself over at this place.

To get law enforcement involved is atrocious. When nincompoops call the cops on you they are actually trying to actively get you into some deep s*** and that's just not right. They have gone to great and ILLEGAL lengths to try to get my family and I into trouble. How can people that do illegal things point their finger at anyone else and no offense but divorced people don't have the right to judge a marriage and there are other illegal things that go on there as well.

Who knows? The next thing could be accusations of child abuse against me or family. Or something showing up on my computer I didn't install. Welcome to the world of gang stalkers. Like I said earlier, they have their objectives. But let's talk about how to deal with it.

First of all stay positive and keep your head up. Just keep trucking. If you need emotional support reach out to me on Facebook, worldwide! I can offer emotional support to you at no charge.
(https://www.facebook.com/chomipraglawoffices?ref=hl)
(https://www.facebook.com/AuthorChomiPrag?ref=hl)

If you are alone, you are at a great disadvantage. You need to try to find someone to double up with. You need to find a partner. I know you don't want to hear that but it would be best if you could find someone to LIVE with. You need someone to stick together with, a person where you watch each other's back. I would like to say that you can do it on your own and you can, but I wouldn't recommend it. You need someone on your side; be it a roommate, a lover, a spouse...someone you can live with. Someone you can trust, someone who's on your side. Targeted individuals can post ads to each other here (http://www.tisclassifieds.com/). You aren't as strong alone; you can tackle it better with someone else.

I would also recommend that you or your partner purchase a gun and learn how to use it to protect yourself and your family. You may not like to hear that but if you are fearful for yourself and your family you have the right to protect yourself. Even if you aren't fearful, you have the right. If a group of people will go so far as to gang up on you and watch your every move and everything you say and try to get you into legal trouble believe me they have no morals and ethics themselves so your life and the life of your family doesn't mean anything to them. If you live in a state that allows carry and conceal and you wish to carry your gun in public with you because you are afraid for your life on the street do so immediately but understand that once you obtain that carry and conceal license you'll lose privacy to the government because you have to tell the government where you live and blah, blah, blah.
(http://www.usacarry.com/concealed_carry_permit_information.html)

In some states you don't have to have a carry and conceal license to take a gun outside the home with you. The police are after the fact and they're not there to save your life. That's what you're there to do. It's your responsibility to take care of your own. If you are thinking of suicide DO NOT BUY A FIREARM WHATSOEVER. You need to get medical attention immediately by calling 911.

It may be easier in some states to obtain a shotgun rather than a

handgun. I mean legally. ☺ Research local laws and the type of firearm you will feel comfortable with.

Don't keep your mouth shut. You're not doing anyone any favors. Be a loud mouth and vocal about what you're going through, it'll protect you in the end. Publicize it, tell others about it, join the Freedom from Covert Harassment group. Mr. Robinson is very helpful and honestly is always there to help gang stalked victims. (https://www.freedomfchs.com/) There's nothing to be ashamed about in life, don't let people put you in a position that they can blackmail you. As long as you're not doing anything illegal you have nothing to worry about. Tell other people, talk about it on Facebook. Even if you are or have done something illegal don't allow yourself to be blackmailed. Contact my law office immediately for help.

These people will try to make you look bad no matter what to other people and everyone else. Your family and friends know who you are and you won't look bad and you don't have anything to prove to them. If people want to make you look bad you have no power or control over it. Just keep moving forward in life. Listen, the attitude that you should have is this: YOU HAVE NO PRIVACY, BUT HOPE THAT YOU DO. So, whatever. Your life will keep moving forward if you keep moving forward. Have this attitude! You don't need to cower and hide.

Fifth, move away. You have a right to move away from your current situation and there's nothing wrong with that. There's legal basis to do so as well. No one can expect you to live with zero privacy so it's time for you to go. Besides, it doesn't matter what other people expect of you. Why pay your money to a place or any business that doesn't appreciate you? That makes no sense. You are in control of your money, YOU. Just quit it and leave if you're suffering from gang stalking where you live.

CHAPTER 7
HOW TO DEFEAT YOUR GANG STALKERS

There is no magical way to defeat your gang stalkers because first of all you have to have a clear mind. This is quite difficult to do when there is so much negativity around you. I hope you have at least ONE person around you can trust. I'm hoping to do another Talk Shoe so people can call in with their stories to get things off their chest. My family and I understand what it's like to live with things bottled up. Victims hearing other victim's stories helps them cope and get through life.

I've had people reach out to me about the hiring of private investigators. They aren't cheap and they can't necessarily find out everything you want to know. Also, honestly, they aren't cheap and may try to gouge you too. Some attorneys do the same. Other targeted individuals have told me they believe the private investigator was actually part of the gang stalking themselves. Damn straight they can be. This is also quite unethical, if that's the case. I wish I had better news for you but I don't. My office can perform background searches and things of that nature, but I don't profess to be a private investigator. It is WRONG to take a person's money and pretend to work for them while working for their enemy or enemies.

"Stalk" the stalkers. I don't mean literally since stalking is illegal. You should take pictures of license plates and find out who the vehicle is registered to. Our office is able to do this for you at a discounted price cheaper than private investigators. It can be very difficult to do these things alone, which is why you'll need help from someone else. Two heads are stronger than one.

Send Open Records/ Freedom of Information requests to obtain information about your stalkers. There are forms for this on the internet, forms particular to your state. Open records requests are state records requests, Freedom of Information requests are federal records requests and there's a lot of information you can get from these! If you're looking for information on your stalkers it's likely you can get that information or at least some information about the stalkers in that fashion.

If you suspect a corporation/ company is involved in illegal wiretapping and eavesdropping, such as Time Warner Cable or one of their employees or any other company such as Vonage or the like, send letters to them directly by getting their general address as well as their legal department's address and send letters reminding them that warrantless wiretapping and eavesdropping is illegal and could involve criminal penalties and punishments. There are also monetary penalties they'll suffer. Make sure you keep a log as to when you called, who you spoke to and what was discussed with them. As a matter of fact if you do this via the "chat" feature make sure to ask them for a copy of the chat transcript. Make sure they email it to you before you log off the chat session and make sure you have that emailed chat session before logging off with them. Go check your inbox while making them wait. Time Warner Cable is notorious for not giving you a copy of your "chat" transcript. Remember, something in writing is better in court than something orally stated. Just one person's word against another's may not be enough. Also complain to the lower level employee and then ask to speak to the supervisor and do the same.

If you're alone say out loud and repeat that "stalking is a crime", because it is, and if you think illegal wiretapping and eavesdropping is being used it'll let your gang stalkers know that you know the law and mean business. Anything they obtain illegally about you can't be used in a court of law and if it's publicized or used it will be obvious that illegal wiretapping and eavesdropping were in fact used against you so they can shoot themselves in their own foot. At best the private information they found out will only be able to stay amongst them. Have you accepted that you have no privacy, none at all? Accept it now and get over it, let's move along.

Conduct "asset protection". There's nothing wrong with protecting your assets, even if you don't have much. Open a business and begin conducting your matter under a business name; Preferably a Limited Liability Company; "LLC". My office can most certainly help you with this! Your matters are more private if you do it under a business name rather than your name personally. Don't set the business up in your name either, use a fictitious name. Limited liability companies are excellent vehicles to do this. Get mail sent to a mailing address, not a US post office box, a PRIVATE mailing address serviced by a private mailing company. Even pay per minute phones aren't necessarily private, but may be the best option for you. Use cash, stay away from credit cards and have zero debt if possible! If you have to use a credit card try to get a pre paid, secured card and use that because hotels may require a credit card is used to at least reserve a room. But even a secured credit card isn't private. Try to purchase things and use a different name as the registered owner; don't use your real name. Please contact my office for more information.

Vary your routine; don't take the same route or routes. Don't use the same stores; the same anything.

Don't be alone, be around people who support and believe you. PEOPLE YOU TRUST. Get a pet. Sometimes it can take some time to find someone to trust, but eventually you'll find them. If there are people around who don't believe you just stop hanging around them. Either someone believes you or they don't. Believe in yourself!

Remember you do need to move on with your life. Do not dwell on the situation.

Leave a paper trail of what's been going on so that there's something in case anything happens to you and your family. You don't know who all may be involved. They'll even go so far as to track you through your vehicle too. Let it be known to others what's going on. Make sure when you do speak to someone you get their name, like the representative's name you spoke to on the phone. If you try to complain later that you spoke to someone, if the company or person is also participating in gang stalking, they'll make up excuses not to take your complaint like "You can't even give me the name of who you spoke to". Yeah; excuses, excuses, excuses. Make sure to keep a track of names, dates, times, license plate numbers, patrol car numbers, police officer's badge numbers and the like.

That's why doing these things alone is hard. Two set of eyes is better than one. If you can, take pictures or videos of your perpetrators, their vehicles and license plate numbers.

Get ready to go to court as your final weapon.

ABOUT THE AUTHOR

Chomi Prag is an attorney who graduated from Syracuse Law School, passed the Wisconsin Bar Exam as well as the Multi-State Professional Responsibility Exam, and is admitted to the United States Supreme Court. Chomi has been self employed for over a decade helping clients in all aspects of the law and educating the general public about their legal rights, especially when it comes to law enforcement and the United States Constitution.

She's considered a whistle blower who helps the downtrodden underdog, and is a strong believer in the right to keep and bear arms as provided in the Second Amendment to the US Constitution, the right to free speech as provided in the First Amendment and the Fourth Amendment right to be free from unreasonable searches and seizures. She was the first person in her family to graduate with a college degree.

Attorney Prag helps "the little guy" and isn't afraid of people, companies, corporations or agencies that use illegal and underhanded tactics to try to "one up" her, her clients and people she cares about. They don't "like" her. Therefore, Chomi Prag, as well as her editor Thomas Carney, have been the target of corrupt law enforcement officials, unlawful and baseless accusations by prosecutors, and unethical actions taken by fraudulent court officials that include court commissioners, judges, court clerks and a tainted judicial commission.

Chomi has practical experience in the field of gang stalking as well as counter surveillance since she is a TARGETED INDIVIDUAL who has had illegal wiretapping and eavesdropping performed on her.

Since trouble follows her wherever she goes her life is filled with drama and interesting experiences that give her the compassion to reach out and help those who are being bullied and attacked by people in authority positions and those less fortunate.

Chomi comes from a blue collar family; her father is a US army veteran from the "Screaming Eagles" 101st Airborne Division and her mother is a devoted homemaker who speaks English as a second language.

She always enjoys a challenge, loves helping others and is in the process of writing a sequel to her first published novel CULT OF MIRRORS. She herself is a TARGETED INDIVIDUAL.